D1083946

Jonathan Edwards

Twayne's United States Authors Series

Patricia Cowell, Editor

Colorado State University

TUSAS 537

Rev. Jonathan Edwards (1703–1758), by Joesph Badger (1708–1765);
courtesy Yale University Art Gallery, bequest of Eugene Phelps Edwards, 1938

Jonathan Edwards

by M. X. Lesser

Northeastern University

Twayne Publishers
A Division of G.K. Hall & Co. • *Boston*

Jonathan Edwards

M. X. Lesser

Copyright 1988 by G.K. Hall & Co.
All rights reserved.
Published by Twayne Publishers
A Division of G.K. Hall & Co.
70 Lincoln Street
Boston, Massachusetts 02111

Copyediting supervised by Barbara Sutton
Book production by Gabrielle B. McDonald
Book design by Barbara Anderson

Typeset in 11 pt. Garamond
by Compset, Inc., Beverly, Massachusetts

Printed on permanent/durable acid-free paper
and bound in the United States of America

Library of Congress Cataloging in Publication Data

Lesser, M. X.
    Jonathan Edwards / by M. X. Lesser.
        p. cm.—(Twayne's United States authors series ; TUSAS 537)
    Bibliography: p.
    Includes index.
    ISBN 0-8057-7519-6 (alk. paper)
    1. Edwards, Jonathan, 1703–1758—Criticism and interpretation.
2. Christian literature, American—History and criticism.
I. Title.   II. Series.
PS742.L47 1988
285.8'092'4—dc19

For Al
who never knew him

Contents

About the Author

M. X. Lesser earned his doctorate at Columbia University—his dissertation was a study of seventeenth-century election sermons—and has taught at the University of Delaware, Rutgers University, and, since 1969, at Northeastern University. He has written articles on American literature and *Jonathan Edwards: A Reference Guide,* an annotated bibliography. His *The Fiction of Experience* was published by McGraw-Hill.

Preface

"He that will know the workings of the mind of New England in the middle of the last century, and the throbbings of its heart," warned the American historian George Bancroft in 1859, "must give his days and nights to the study of Jonathan Edwards."[1] Aside from its tight schedule, Bancroft's encomium slights another cultural hero of the time, Benjamin Franklin. Born in Boston just three years after Edwards, Franklin shared half a century with him and a common affection for George Whitefield, the great preacher of the Great Awakening. Edwards, Whitefield tells us, wept at his exhortations; Franklin emptied his purse. Franklin knew Edwards and published him. "Read the Pages of Mr. Edwards' late Book" on moral duty, he advised his sister Jenny.[2] Edwards, as far as the records go, never knew Franklin nor advised any of his ten sisters to read the Widow Silence Dogood on anything. To describe, let alone to know, the mind and heart of New England in the middle of the eighteenth century requires at least both Edwards and Franklin, the minister of Northampton, Massachusetts, and the minister to France, the authors, in the same year, of *Original Sin* and *The Way to Wealth*. To read Edwards is to read but half the story, a necessary half and, it seems to me, a remarkably consistent one in a time of profound change.[3]

A few months before he died, Edwards wrote the trustees of Princeton that his mind was so "swallowed up" with theological projects of one sort or another—a history of redemption particularly, "a Body of Divinity in an entire new method"—that he might reject their offer of the college presidency.[4] No phrase better captures the whole of Edwards's theological enterprise than that, a new way of doing old religion. It characterizes not only his history of redemption, but his sermon on divine light as well; his treatise on the affections, and his inquiry into the will; his defense of original sin, and his dissertation on true virtue. In one way or another, all these works celebrate his "*delightful* conviction" of the absolute sovereignty of God and the "new sense" of things he first discovered at conversion. The end for which God created the world, he wrote in 1755, was God Himself. It is all of a piece.

Edwards's assumptions were founded on doctrinal orthodoxy—on divine sovereignty and original sin and free grace; freshened by contemporary philosophical thought from abroad—by Isaac Newton, John Locke, and Francis Hutcheson, among others; challenged by the realities of a New England parish nearing mid-century—by "bad" books and shifts in authority; and submitted to a logic unremitting and unforgiving. He wrote and published, as thoroughly as long hours and a shortened life would allow, a rational and inventive account, a strict and lively orthodoxy. He became, even in his day, the articulate voice of a creed outworn, dismissed by his congregation, exiled to a frontier settlement. An historical artifact, the nineteenth century thought. Still, the keepers of heart religion and the askers after human frailty may yet give themselves to the study of Edwards, if not days and nights, then hours certainly.

This study attempts to trace Edwards's thought as a connected series of comments on the doctrine of divine sovereignty, from his early speculative papers on spiders and being through his published sermons on justification and charity to his formal treatises on free will and original sin. That doctrine is the "awful sweetness" that permeates his conversion experience, his imprecatory sermons, his evangelical ardor, and his millennial hope. It also accounts in part for the struggle Edwards had with the limits of language, a point of increasing importance to him and, so, to this study. The first chapter recounts his life through letters, diaries, journals, resolutions, his conversion narrative, and his farewell sermon; the second chapter examines his scientific and philosophical beginnings detailed in notebooks, marginalia, and miscellanies; the third chapter sketches his first years at Northampton and his pastoral round of sermons; the fourth chapter reports the Great Awakening, his role in it, his analysis of it, and its consequences for him; the fifth chapter takes up the Stockbridge years of his unfinished body of divinity; and the sixth chapter gauges his critical reception. For texts, I use the Yale Edwards and follow its editors to the Worcester (1808) and New York (1829) "complete" editions for texts not yet edited by them.

Even as slim a volume as this rests upon many acts of kindness; recalling them doubles the happy debt. I would like to thank especially Jon Lanham of Harvard for ploughing through line after stout line; Guy Rotella of Northeastern for listening to the most of it; the librarians at Gordon-Conwell, Yale, and Harvard, particularly Ed Doctoroff of Widener, for easing the way; and to Lisa Steves for making good sense of a difficult hand.

To the Brownie and the kids down the lane—Meg, Peter, and Jo— I owe more than thanks for keeping the faith.

M. X. Lesser

Northeastern University

Chronology

1738   *Discourses on Various Important Subjects.* Preaches on charity and its fruits.

1739   "Personal Narrative." Preaches on the history of redemption.

1740   The Great Awakening: George Whitefield preaches at Northampton in October.

1741   8 July, *Sinners in the Hands of an Angry God.* 2 September, *Resort and Remedy.* 10 September, *Distinguishing Marks,* the Yale commencement address.

1742   Preaches on religious affections.

1743   *Some Thoughts Concerning the Present Revival. Great Concern.*

1744   *True Excellency.*

1746   *Religious Affections. The Church's Marriage.*

1747   *True Saints.*

1748   *Humble Attempt. A Strong Rod.*

1749   *Life of Brainerd. Humble Inquiry. Christ the Great Example.*

1750   22 June, dismissed by his congregation. 2 July, preaches farewell sermon. Writes "Preface," for *True Religion Delineated,* by Joseph Bellamy.

1751   *A Farewell Sermon.* 8 August, installed pastor and missionary to the Indians, Stockbridge, Massachusetts.

1752   *Misrepresentations Corrected.*

1753   *True Grace.*

1754   *Freedom of the Will.*

1755   Drafts dissertations on the end of the world and true virtue.

1757   Completes manuscript on original sin. Chosen president of Princeton.

1758   16 February, inducted president. 22 March, dies of smallpox. *Original Sin.*

1765   "Personal Narrative," in Samuel Hopkins, *The Life of Edwards. Two Dissertations.*

1774   *A History of the Work of Redemption.*

1780   *Sermons on the Following Subjects.*

1788   *Practical Sermons.*

1793   *Miscellaneous Observations.*

1806   *The Works of President Edwards* (Leeds, England).

1808   *The Works of President Edwards* (Worcester, Massachusetts).

1829   *The Life of President Edwards,* by Sereno Edwards Dwight; reprints "Resolutions" and "Diary" complete, letters, Edwards's account of his dismissal, etc.

1852   *Charity and Its Fruits.*

1903   *An Unpublished Essay of Edwards on the Trinity.*

1948   *Images or Shadows of Divine Things.*

1957–1985   *The Works of Jonathan Edwards* (Yale), v. 1–7.

Chapter One
A Personal Narrative

In 1739, when he was thirty-six years old, by then the father of five daughters and a son, the minister for ten years of the most important church west of Boston, and the author of a widely read narrative about a religious revival that swept the town five years earlier, Jonathan Edwards wrote a brief account of his life for "his own private advantage."[1] Except for some few letters—one, for example, about his reluctance to become president of Princeton—and a diary he kept intermittently for about a dozen years, "Personal Narrative" is the chief source of Edwards on himself. Like other autobiographies of the time, it records a spiritual progress but leaves unremarked the memories and anecdotes of another life. Still, it touches Edwards at the points of his own choosing, and it is there that for him his life begins.

"From my childhood up," he writes, "my mind had been full of objections against the doctrine of God's sovereignty, in choosing whom he would to eternal life and rejecting whom he pleased; leaving them eternally to perish, and be everlastingly tormented in hell." This basic tenet of Calvinism appeared to him "like a horrible doctrine," but later he had a conviction of the "justice and reasonableness" of it; and later still, when he was seventeen, just after an attack of pleurisy, which shook him "over the pit of hell," he had "not only a conviction, but a *delightful* conviction" of God's absolute sovereignty. He remembers reading 1 Tim. 1:17: "Now unto the King eternal, immortal, invisible, the only wise God, be honor and glory for ever and ever." "As I read the words, there came into my soul, and was as it were diffused thro' it, a sense of the glory of the Divine Being; a new sense, quite different from any thing I ever experienced before." The effect was immediate and profound: he felt an "inward sweetness, . . . a kind of vision . . . [of] sweetly conversing with Christ, and wrapt and swallowed up in God," and soon afterward he told his father of it.

I was pretty much affected by the discourse we had together. And when the discourse was ended, I walked abroad alone, in a solitary place in my father's

1

pasture, for contemplation. And as I was walking there, and looked up on the sky and clouds; there came into my mind, a sweet sense of the glorious majesty and grace of God, that I know not how to express. I seemed to see them both in a sweet conjunction: majesty and meekness join'd together: it was a sweet and gentle, and holy majesty; and also a majestic meekness; an awful sweetness; a high, and great, and holy gentleness.

All the world changed then, "every thing was altered" by divine, sweet glory: the sun, the moon, and the stars; the grass, the flowers, and the trees; the waters and the clouds. The frontier world he knew from childhood, the meadows and the woods and the river, changed. Even thunder changed: "I used to be a person uncommonly terrified with thunder. . . . But now, on the contrary, it rejoiced me."[2]

This new sense of things, inexpressible then in all but its effects, never left him. Throughout his life he would return to the world of nature, solitary on foot or horseback, to resume the old devotions. And whatever he was later to urge in matters of faith or matters of reason, in miscellanies or sermons or treatises, was fixed upon that still point of God's absolute sovereignty, discovered in piety and love and beauty. It was the fact of his life no less than his work.

The Early Years

Heart and mind prepared. Jonathan Edwards was born on 5 October 1703, in East Windsor, Connecticut.[3] The fifth child and only son among ten daughters of Timothy and Esther Stoddard Edwards, the young Edwards could hardly avoid his calling. His father, graduated from Harvard and married in 1694, had been pastor of the Connecticut River village for nine years; he would tend his small congregation for another fifty-four years, dying at eighty-nine, two months before his son. His mother, the pious daughter and granddaughter of ministers, lived to be ninety-eight, a woman of wit and beauty. Solomon Stoddard, her father, was minister to the congregation at Northampton for fifty-seven years, patriarch of an aristocratic line. At his death in 1729—he was eighty-seven—his grandson succeeded him.

Edwards was tutored by his father in the family parlor, joined there by his sisters and his friends, conjugating Latin when he was six, Hebrew and Greek somewhat later. When the elder Edwards, chaplain to a Connecticut detachment, left on a military expedition to Canada, the schoolroom tasks (and discipline) fell to his wife. "I desire thee," he writes from New Haven on 7 August 1711, "to take care that Jonathan dont Loose what he hath Learned but that as he has got the accidence, & above two sides of *propria Quae moribus* by heart so that he keep what he hath got, I would therefore have him Say pretty often to the Girls. . . . I hope thou wilt take Special care of Jonathan that he dont be rude & naught &c. of which thee and I have Lately Discoursed."[4]

The boy was a solitary figure, tall and spare—in time, six-foot-one—given to lonely retreats and holy reports. When he was eight or so, he was "very much affected" by a "remarkable awakening" in his father's church. He prayed "five times a day in secret," met with friends for "religious talk," and later with them "built a booth in a deep swamp" for prayers.[5] Four years later, in the earliest extant manuscript in his hand, a letter to his married sister Mary, he tells of "a verry Remarkable stirring and pouring out of the Spirrit of God," then of the deaths of five townsfolk, next of an outbreak of chicken pox among his sisters, and finally of his troubling toothache.[6] Such a pattern of concern—God, community, family, self—first expressed on 10 May 1716, lasted a lifetime. In September of that year he went off to Yale; he was not quite thirteen.

Though not much older than Edwards nor much larger than his family, the college was wracked with discontent and sectional rivalry. Founded in 1701 as an orthodox alternative to liberal Harvard, the Collegiate School had four campuses when Edwards and nine others met to begin their studies under the direction of his young cousin Elisha Williams in Wethersfield, a town not ten miles from his home. He flourished there. As Timothy Cutler, rector of the college, later reported to his father, the boy showed "promising Abilitys and Advances in Learning."[7] Those advances were made in a curriculum very much like Harvard's a decade earlier, and may have included many of the same texts: the logic of Antoine Arnauld and Pierre Nicole; the metaphysics of Henry More, Adrian Heereboord, and Jean LeClerc; the ethics of More and Heereboord; the rational physics of René Descartes; the astronomy of Pierre Gassendi; and the experimental science of Charles Morton. He probably read Isaac Newton's *Principia* (1687) in Samuel Clarke's formulation then and later, probably during his graduate years, John Locke's *An Essay Concerning Human Understanding* (1690).[8]

Edwards was a grave student, bookish, removed from the din of campus life. Writing to his father on the "Preciousness of my time," he notes his "great Content" at the new rector's iron management of the college.[9] He settles a quarrel with his younger roommate (and cousin) by writing of it to his father,[10] and ends a long account of a student protest against school food with this disclaimer, again to his father: "I must needs say for my Own part, that although the Commons at some-times have not been sufficient as to quality, yet I think there has been very little Occasion for such an Insurrection as this." Nor does stealing, card-playing, window-breaking, "Cursing, Swearing, and Damning" among the young seminarians distress him overmuch. "Through the goodness of God I am perfectly free of all their janglings."[11]

Apparently he was, for it is during this time, the early 1720s, that Edwards begins his first speculative papers—"Of Insects," "Natural Philosophy," "Miscellanies," "The Mind," "Notes on Scriptures," and "Notes on the Apocalypse"—and on 31 October 1723, "publishes" his observations on flying spiders in a letter to Judge Paul Dudley of Massachusetts, a colonial fellow of the Royal Society of London and a correspondent of his father. Edwards saw no conflict in these pursuits, at once scientific and biblical, for he took all thought to be one in the transforming light of grace. Such were his joys, he writes in "Personal Narrative," that the soul "appear'd like such a little white flower, as we see in the spring of the year; low and humble on the ground, opening its bosom, to receive the pleasant beams of the sun's glory; rejoicing as it were, in a calm rapture; diffusing around a sweet fragrancy; standing peacefully and lovingly, in the midst of other flowers round about; all in like manner opening their bosoms, to drink in the light of the sun."[12] That extended metaphor hints at his synoptic ways, not only in brief, here and in the notes he kept throughout his life on the natural images of divine things, but also at large, in the easy shift from natural science to theology and back again.

By September 1720 Edwards was graduated—first in his class—but he stayed on at New Haven to prepare for the ministry. When he was eighteen, about a year and a half after he discovered the "new sense" of things, he accepted a call from a small Scots Presbyterian church on William Street, near Wall, in New York.[13] It was there, in the late summer of 1722, that his soul "eagerly catch'd" at Christ's kingdom, animating and refreshing him. He "very frequently used to retire into a solitary place, on the banks of Hudson's river, at some distance from the city, for contemplation of divine things, and secret converse with

God; and had many sweet hours there." But he left in April of the following year to accept a call to the Congregational church in Bolton, Connecticut, remembering later "many sweet and pleasant days" and a "most bitter parting" from his friend of eight months, John Smith, a currier, and his devout mother. On the voyage home he kept the sabbath at Saybrook, where he had "a sweet and refreshing season, walking alone in the fields."[14] Once home, he finished his master's thesis and prepared for the Bolton settlement, but in November Yale offered him a tutorship, and he took it. In time he would become the senior tutor—in effect, the president—of the college and its sixty students.

Resolutions and uncertainties. Many of the resolutions he wrote and much of the diary he kept date from the beginning of his New York pastorate to shortly before he took up his duties in New Haven, a period of something less than two years.[15] First, Edwards cautions himself to "remember to read over these resolutions once a week" much as Benjamin Franklin does at about the same time. Like Franklin, Edwards follows it with instructions to himself that speak of thrift and charity, of temperance and improvement.

5 *Resolved,* Never to lose one moment of time, but to improve it in the most profitable way I possibly can.

13 *Resolved,* To be endeavouring to find out fit objects of charity and liberality.

20 *Resolved,* To maintain the strictest temperance, in eating and drinking.

41 *Resolved,* To ask myself, at the end of every day, week, month and year, wherein I could possibly, in any respect, have done better. *Jan.* 11, 1723.

69 *Resolved,* Always to do that, which I shall wish I had done when I see others do it. *Aug.* 11, 1723.

But Edwards, unlike Franklin, resolves everything in the service of God, for, as he writes in the preface, he is "unable to do anything without God's help." His first resolution provides the context for the remaining sixty-nine:

1 *Resolved,* that *I will do whatsoever* I think to be most to the glory of God and my own good, profit and pleasure, in the whole of my duration; without any consideration of the time, whether now, or never so many myriads of ages hence. Resolved to do whatever I think to be my *duty,* and most for the good and advantage of mankind in general. Resolved, so

to do, whatever *difficulties* I meet with, how many soever, and how great soever.

Resolution 4 (and 23) repeats that sentiment: "Never *to do* any manner of thing, whether in soul or body, less or more, but what tends to the glory of God, not *be,* nor *suffer* it, if I can possibly avoid it." Sin and death figure importantly and, of course, religion.

44 *Resolved,* That no other end but religion, shall have any influence at all on any of my actions; and that no action shall be, in the least circumstance, any otherwise than the religious end will carry it. *Jan.* 12, 1723.

The labor of discipline goes on in a different form when, on Tuesday, 18 December 1722, the occasion of his thirty-fifth resolution, Edwards begins to keep a diary. Gone now are the promises of the "Resolutions" and the heady times of the "Personal Narrative"; the "Diary" chants a litany of self-doubt.

Dec. 18. This day made the 35th Resolution. The reason why I, in the least, question my interest in God's love and favour, is,—1. Because I cannot speak so fully to my experience of that preparatory work, of which divines speak:— 2. I do not remember that I experienced regeneration, exactly in those steps, in which divines say it is generally wrought:—3. I do not feel the christian graces sensibly enough, particularly faith. I fear they are only such hypocritical outside affections, which wicked men may feel, as well as others. They do not seem to be sufficiently inward, full, sincere, entire and hearty. They do not seem so substantial, and so wrought out in my very nature, as I could wish.— 4. Because I am sometimes guilty of sins of omission and commission. Lately I have doubted, whether I do not transgress in evil speaking. This day, re-solved, No.

On Thursday, 20 December, he "somewhat questioned" his negligence; on Friday, he was "dull, dry and dead"; on Saturday, he was "revived." But a week later, 29 December, he was again "dull and lifeless"; his making resolutions, he confides, is "all nothing." At the end of the first week of the new year, he vows "to live in continual mortification, without ceasing, and even to weary myself thereby, as long as I am in this world, and never to expect or desire any worldly ease or pleasure." By mid-February he speaks of renewal, a week later, of negligence; March begins in humility and ends in gluttony. When he is "violently beset with temptation," he confesses on 27 July 1723, he does "some sum in Arithmetic, or Geometry."

The week after he begins his tutorship at Yale in late spring 1724 is "very remarkable," full of "despondencies, fears, perplexities, multitudes of cares, and distraction of mind": he is convinced "of the troublesomeness and vexation of the world, and that it will never be another kind of world." That September "the hurries of commencement" bring on a deep "sinking" within him. The following commencement finds him so seriously ill that he is confined to bed in New Haven for three months, tended by his mother and visited by God: "And when the light of the morning came, and the beams of the sun came in at the window, it refreshed my soul from one morning to another. It seemed to me to be some image of the sweet light of God's glory." His third commencement, on 26 September 1726, stirs the memory of the "low, sunk estate" of the other two. After that, the diary trails off to five more entries over the next nine years, for Edwards had other things to think about, still others to record. That fall he had been invited to the church at Northampton as a colleague of his aging grandfather. On 15 February 1727, he was ordained: he was twenty-three, Solomon Stoddard, eighty-four.

An uncommon union.   Five months later, on 28 July 1727, he married Sarah Pierrepont, a young woman of seventeen, the daughter of one of the founders of Yale and the great-granddaughter of the founder of Hartford and the Connecticut church, Thomas Hooker. Four years earlier, when he was twenty and she was thirteen, he jotted down his impressions of her in many of the same words he later would use about his conversion, a language compounded in love. God "fills her mind with exceeding sweet delight," and she fully "expects after a while to be received up where he is," there "to be ravished with his love and delight forever." She has a "strange sweetness," a "wonderful sweetness, calmness and universal benevolence of mind." She goes "from place to place, singing sweetly; and seems to be always full of joy and pleasure; and no one knows for what. She loves to be alone, walking in the fields and groves, and seems to have some one invisible always conversing with her."[16] Their "uncommon union," as Edwards called it, lasted thirty years. They were by all accounts (and in the surviving portraits) a striking couple, tall and imperial, and in manner complementary, her ease tempering his reserve. Uncomfortable with the idle chat of his parishioners, Edwards counted on Sarah to carry him through, her wit and charm to close the distance. An English visitor thought her a woman "adorn'd with a meek and quiet Spirit," who "talked feelingly and solidly of the Things of God," "the very Daughter of *Abraham*" he wished for himself.[17] She bore eleven children—the first, Sarah, on a Sabbath, 25 August 1728—and managed the family cares with skill. As he confessed once in her absence, "We have been without [yo]u almost as long as we know how to [be]."[18]

Edwards, a contemporary reports, "commonly spent thirteen hours every day in his study," rising at four on summer days, at five in the chill of the Northampton winter.[19] He wrote on anything that came to hand—backs of invitations, invoices, cuttings from fans. After lunch in summer he usually rode alone through the woods behind their King Street home, stopping to scribble some part of an idea on paper slips he carried with him, pinning them to his coat, moving on within their flutterings. Many saw their way into his miscellanies—a journal he began at Yale that grew to nearly 1400 items and nine volumes in forty years—and ultimately into the thousand sermons he preached and the half dozen treatises he wrote during his lifetime. In winter he chopped wood.

Pastoral Letters

First lecture, first harvest. When Solomon Stoddard died on 11 February 1729, Edwards became pastor to the congregation of six hundred at a salary of £200, but he was forced to leave the pulpit that spring, a victim of an illness every bit as debilitating as the one he had suffered at Yale. He regained his health—a frail thing at best—by early fall and took up his pastoral duties once more. Within two years, when he was twenty-seven, he was invited to Boston for his first public lecture, a stunning (and orthodox) defense of divine sovereignty. *God Glorified* (1731) was published "at the desire of several ministers" and in hopes that the principles of his grandfather would "shine" in him.[20] By later 1733, it was evident that they would.

Over the course of his long ministry, Solomon Stoddard reaped several "harvests" of the repentant—in 1679, 1683, 1690, 1712, and 1718. Now Edwards, faced with much the same "looseness," exhorted his people, especially the young, to pray for change. They answered with group prayer meetings held in their homes, a practice that spread quickly and solemnly to their elders. By the end of 1734, five or six suddenly converted, among them "one of the greatest company-keepers in the whole town."[21] By early spring, the number swelled to thirty a week, touching the smaller towns in the Valley; by June, Edwards's uncle, Joseph Hawley, brought to soul despair, "Laid violent Hands on himself, & Put an End to his Life, by Cutting his own throat";[22] by December, the town once again slipped into spiritual lethargy. The surprising conversions were history; all they lacked was an historian.

Learning of the Northampton revival, the respected minister of the Brattle Street Church in Boston prevailed upon Edwards to write an account of it. The narrative, an eight-page letter written in late spring 1735 (and expanded considerably a year and a half later in a second letter), found willing readers among the Rev. Dr. Benjamin Colman's London correspondents. Colman published a nineteen-page abridgement of the second letter in Boston in December 1736; the unabridged London text, which runs to 132 pages, was published in 1737. *A Faithful Narrative* established Edwards's reputation among evangelicals abroad—in Scotland, the Netherlands, Germany—as the pious recorder of revivals in New England. Closer home, he recorded another surprising work of God.

On 13 March 1737, just as he began his Sunday sermon, the gallery of the old church on Meetinghouse Hill collapsed, spilling people and timbers upon some seventy women and children in the "middle alley" below. "But so mysteriously and wonderfully did it come to pass, that every life was preserved." It was for Edwards and his congregation a "sufficient argument" of divine providence. They met again that Wednesday in humble prayer, mindful, as their pastor noted, of the spirit of God still upon them, a preservation and a rebuke.[23]

The following year *Discourses on Various Important Subjects* (1738) was published "at the desire and expense of the town," a series of five sermons preached "chiefly" during the Northampton "outpouring." The text includes, first and enlarged, "Justification by Faith Alone"; then, "Pressing into the Kingdom of God," "Ruth's Resolution," and "The Justice of God in the Damnation of Sinners"; and, last, "The Excellency of Jesus Christ," a sermon not originally in the series but, Edwards thought, "proper" to its theme.[24] Proper as well, though again not quite part of it, was the earlier *A Divine and Supernatural Light* (1734), an attempt to distinguish the true spirit of God from the false. By 1740, Edwards and Northampton, indeed much of the east coast of America, were caught up in that vexing problem.

In defense of passion. The Great Awakening, as it came to be called, began in earnest with the arrival in Boston on 18 September 1740, of the English Methodist, George Whitefield. There had been seasons of revivals before—those of Theodorus Frelinghausen among German pietists in New Jersey a decade earlier, for one—but they were as gentle rain to the fitful storms Whitefield wrought. Up and down the eastern seaboard he preached, his pulpit eloquence "a wonderful power over the hearts and purses of his hearers" from New England to Georgia. In Philadelphia, Ben Franklin, listening to Whitefield, "silently resolved" to keep his coins from him. "As he proceeded I began to soften, and concluded to give the Coppers. Another Stroke of his Oratory made me asham'd of that, and determin'd me to give the Silver; and he finish'd so admirably, that I empty'd my Pocket wholly into the Collector's Dish, Gold and all."[25] In Northampton, after a long weekend of preaching in late October, Whitefield confided to his journal that "good Mr. Edwards wept during the whole time of the exercise" on Sunday morning.[26] The next day Edwards rode out the Boston road with him as far as East Windsor, returning alone to Northampton and the anguished cries of the repentant. Springtime saw no relief.

On 8 July 1741, Edwards preached at Enfield, Connecticut, invited there at the last minute. To that congregation as to his own, his "appearance, his countenance, words and whole demeanor . . . was attended with a seriousness, gravity and solemnity." He read from a prepared text, as was his practice then, and spoke with his usual "clearness and precision," "without much noise or external emotion."[27] And, as always, he "used no gestures, but looked straight forward," looked, as one of his parishioners remarked, "'on the bell rope until he looked it off.'"[28] Halfway through the sermon "there was a great moaning & crying out through the whole House." He stopped, then began again, but soon the "shrieks & crys were piercing & Amazing."[29] Stillness then, his last words—"'Haste and escape for your lives, look not behind you. Escape to the mountain, lest you be consumed'"—a prayer, a hymn, and the congregation filed out. The text Edwards developed was from Deut. 32:35, "Their foot shall slide in due time"; the sermon, *Sinners in the Hands of an Angry God.*[30] Publication later that year of perhaps the most famous sermon in American pulpit history marks the apogee of the Great Awakening, for shortly afterwards Boston and much of New England turned increasingly from such doleful imprecations, Old Lights against the New Lights of revivalism. Whitefield was discredited, other itinerants publicly rejected. By August 1742 the Massachusetts Judicial Court declared James Davenport, the most fiery among them, mad.

Against this rising discontent Edwards published three books in rapid order. *Distinguishing Marks* (1741), the Yale commencement address of 10 September 1741, so impressed the undergraduates that one, Samuel Hopkins, undertook studies with Edwards and became, in time, his theological successor; the faculty, somewhat less impressed, never invited him to speak there again. *Some Thoughts Concerning the Present Revival* (1743), a spirited defense of all but the most extravagant excesses of the Awakening, records his wife's religious ecstasies. *Religious Affections* (1746), reworked from a series of lectures Edwards gave in the winter of 1743, probes (and sanctions) emotion in religion and is, before William James, the definitive psychological analysis of the religious experience. During the same five years, Edwards published a funeral sermon for his uncle, William Williams; two ordination sermons, one for Jonathan Judd of Northampton and the other for Robert Abercrombie of Pelham; two pamphlets refuting charges of conspiracy raised against him by the rector of Yale; and an installation sermon for Samuel Buell of Easthampton, a young minister who took over the Northampton pulpit during Edwards's forays among the unconverted in neighboring towns and who stood by Sarah in her spiritual trials.[31] In early 1748, Edwards joined a group of Scots ministers in supporting a worldwide concert of prayer and published *Humble Attempt.*

Discord and early sorrow.   For all that, Edwards was quickly losing favor. From the beginning of his pastorate, the river merchants of the town resented his magisterial ways and the deeded authority of his pulpit.[32] His grandfather apparently knew how to handle them, for he moved among his merchant kings "pope" of the Connecticut Valley. A generation earlier, Edwards's aunts—daughters of the venerable Stoddard—married into the influential Williamses and Hawleys. But the grandson had few of the old man's gifts of compromise, fewer daughters of marrying age. As the fires of the Great Awakening died, the resentment of the merchants quickened, and by the spring of 1744 they openly challenged him as he reached for their money, their children, and their unregenerate souls.

First, Edwards asked, no less than four times, for a fixed salary instead of the usual drafts for debts incurred. They refused. In March, his wife pleaded with the town constable to send some money "as much as you Possibbly can for Mr Edwards is under Such obligations that he cant Possibbly do without it."[33] Whatever the town did with that request, it did not grant him a fixed salary for another three years and then only after public, and often humiliating, budget hearings.

Second, he brought their resentment home. After services one Sunday in March, Edwards reported high mischief in the making: several young people were suspected of reading and distributing a "bad book"; *The Midwife Rightly Instructed,* it turned out to be.[34] Referred to mockingly as the "young folks' Bible" by one of its more avid readers, the birthing manual turned pornographic in their hands. Edwards called for a committee to investigate the matter, got it, and then, before the benediction, read aloud the names of the sons and daughters of the best pews, the accused and the witnesses alike. "When the names were published, it appeared, that there were but few of the considerable families in town to which none of the persons named did belong, or were nearly related. Whether this was the occasion of the alteration or not, before the day appointed came, a great number of heads of families altered their minds (yea many condemned what they had done, before they got home to their own houses) and declared, they did not think proper to proceed as they had done; that their children should not be called to an account in such a way for such things, etc. etc.; and the town was suddenly all on a blaze."[35] By 3 June, the culprits—all three of them—confessed, though not before damning with contempt and insolence the authority of minister and pulpit. Their elders were inclined to agree with them, point and tone.

Third, Edwards changed the terms of full church membership by insisting that candidates make a public profession of sanctifying grace before taking communion, a practice formally abandoned by his grandfather some forty years before and enjoined by Edwards in the twenty-three years of his pastorate.[36] Stoddard not only adopted the liberal Half-Way Covenant—a doctrine of church membership drawn up by a synod of ministers in 1662—but went a step further by making the Lord's Supper a converting ordinance open to all but the most scandalous.

Mr. Edwards had some hesitation about this matter when he first settled at Northampton, and afterwards; but did not receive such a degree of conviction, that the admitting persons into the church, who made no pretense to real godliness was wrong, as to prevent his practicing upon it with a good conscience, for some years. But at length his doubts about the matter greatly increased, which put him upon examining it more thoroughly than he had ever before done, by searching the Scripture, and reading and examining such books, as were written to defend the admission of persons to sacraments, without a profession of saving faith. And the result was a full conviction that it was wrong, and, that he could not practice upon it with a good conscience.

So deep was the offense that "the general cry was to have him dismissed."[37] But no candidate for admission came forward, and for a time pastor and people were saved from themselves. Besides, the grief arising from the French and Indian War drove problems of church polity from them, what with their sons and brothers off in Cape Breton. For him, sorrow lay much closer.

On 9 October 1747, just four days after Edwards's forty-fourth birthday, David Brainerd, a young minister he had befriended, died of tuberculosis in his King Street home. Edwards had first met him at the 1743 Yale commencement when Brainerd attempted a reconciliation with the faculty that had expelled him in his sophomore year for "some indiscreet remarks" about a tutor's opposition to Whitefield's preaching there during the height of the Great Awakening. Brainerd was moved by the older man's strong defense and wise counsel; Edwards, for his part, admired the young man's "great degree of calmness and humility" in the face of Yale's denial of a degree.[38] In March 1747, Brainerd left his Indian mission in New Jersey at the onset of his illness and returned to New England and eventually to Northampton in late July, nursed by Edwards's second daughter, Jerusha. He died there two months later: he was twenty-nine. Edwards delivered the funeral sermon, *True Saints* (1747), and two years later published parts of a diary and a memoir, *Life of Brainerd* (1749).

On Sunday, 14 February, Jerusha died of a tubercular infection: she was seventeen. A week later her father delivered the eulogy drawn from Job 14:2, "He cometh forth like a flower and is cut down." Edwards spoke of "'My own dear Child,'" offered thanks to those parishioners before him who had "'shown affection on [the] occasion of her death,'" and prayed that the "happy Consequence" of "'my own Loss'" would be a spiritual awakening among the young.[39] By late summer he writes a friend in Scotland of his "great loss," thinking Jerusha "the flower of the family" still.[40] By year's end what remained of the town's sympathy turned to ashes as the controversy over admissions flared up again.

On his dismissal.   In December, after a four-year hiatus, a candidate for church membership finally appeared: Edwards refused him admission without a public profession. In February, he drafted a version of an acceptable profession for another candidate, Mary Hulbert. As Edwards recounts the incident in a journal he kept during those difficult times,[41] "She declared herself ready to own that profession, but said that she was afraid, by what she had heard, that there would be a tumult." Yet she agreed to go forward with it if, as he proposed, the committee of the church consented. It refused; a week later it refused him the pulpit to speak upon it. About the middle of April he vowed to "resign the ministry over this church" if it were unconvinced by his reasons for a public profession in the forthcoming *Humble Inquiry* (1749). After what seemed to the town an unconscionable delay, his 136-page scriptural defense appeared that August in Boston: it was not "generally read" in Northampton nor, he added, "likely to be." By mid-October, eleven of his noisy critics—the Pomeroys, the Lymans, the Wrights, the Hunts—met to form a precinct committee "'to endeavor after a separation'" of pastor and people, thus usurping the authority of the standing committee of the church proper. Their actions, Edwards warned, tended "to make void all the power of churches, and to render church meetings a mere nullity, and to set Pastor aside altogether as a cypher." Heedless of that and of his lengthy written objections, they resolved that he leave. "'Whereas our Pastor, the Rev. Mr. Edwards, having separated and departed from the principles which the great Mr. Stoddard brought in and practised, and which he himself was settled upon, and a long time practised, with respect to the admission of members in complete standing into the visible Church, whether it be not the opinion of the Church, that those principles are inconsistent with the principles of religion, and the peace of Church and Town, and therefore desire a separation, he continuing in his principles.'"

To that end, the church met again and again, and on 16 December, "after long debating and much earnest talk till after sun-down," they voted to call a council of neighboring churches to advise them how best to conduct the affair. But the preparatory council, as it was called, failed Edwards's critics, for it recommended that "Pastor and People should converse freely together"; that there be "no *public* proceedings of any kind whatever, relative to the point in controversy"; and that "one probable occasion of the great uneasiness" was the refusal to hear him from the pulpit. Encouraged, he declared his intention to preach on lecture days—Thursdays—until he had explained himself to his people and, despite efforts of the precinct committee to persuade him otherwise, delivered his first lecture on 16 February. It was "thinly attended" by the townsfolk, as were the remaining four lectures, but there was "a very great number of strangers," he notes, "much more than half the Congregation." On 2 April, the precinct committee wrote the Hampshire County Association of Churches for advice on the composition of a definitive council to adjudicate the problem of separation. That day Edwards wrote the Rev. Mr. Thomas Gillespie of Carnock, Scotland, "I am going to be cast on the wide world, with my large family of ten children—I humbly request your prayers for me under my difficulties and trials."[42]

Within a month both minister and committee settled on ten churches (and ministers), each to choose five, both within the county and without, but only nine ministers convened: one of Edwards's nominees "did not see fit to join the council."[43] Joseph Hawley, a young lawyer and cousin of Edwards, nominated Robert Breck, pastor of Springfield. Fifteen years earlier, when Hawley was a boy of eleven, his father killed himself during Edwards's Northampton revival. That same year the Hampshire Association of ministers refused to ordain Breck because of his "youthful immorality, and anti-scriptural [Arminian] tenets,"[44] and, on his appeal to a Boston council of ministers, had him jailed. The Massachusetts General Assembly censured the Association; Breck was finally ordained, and Edwards, who took no part in the quarrel, was asked by his uncle, the Rev. Mr. William Williams of Hatfield, to write a defense of the Association's decision. Nearly two years later he published a reply, which quickly (and permanently) alienated Breck and a host of his supporters. Thus, when the Council met to begin its deliberations on 19 June 1750, not only was it unevenly divided, but both its local advocate for separation and one of its delegates harbored personal, long-standing grievances against Edwards. The results, three days later, surprised no one.

By a vote of five to four, the Council recommended that inasmuch as "the Rev. Mr. Edwards, persisting in his principles, and the church in theirs" it was both "necessary" and "expedient" that "the relation between pastor and people . . . be immediately dissolved."[45] On hearing the verdict in the church assembled, the people "zealously voted" to dismiss their pastor, 200 to 20.[46] On Sunday, 2 July, almost nine years to the day of his triumph at Enfield, Edwards took leave of his flock. He reminded them, in the doctrine of his farewell sermon, that "'Ministers, and people that are under his care, must meet one another before Christ's tribunal at the day of judgment.'" He recalls his time with them, his labors and his loss:

It was three and twenty years, the 15th day of last February, since I have labored in the work of the ministry, in the relation of a pastor to this church and congregation. . . . I have spent the prime of my life and strength in labors for your eternal welfare. You are my witnesses, that what strength I have had I have not neglected in idleness, nor laid out in prosecuting worldly schemes, and managing temporal affairs, for the advancement of my outward estate, and aggrandizing myself and family; but have given myself wholly to the work of the ministry, laboring in it night and day, rising early and applying myself to this great business to which Christ appointed me. . . . But now I have reason to think my work is finished which I had to do as your minister: You have publicly rejected me, and my opportunities cease.

He regrets such a "melancholy parting," leaving a "gall of bitterness" behind, leaving God's work undone, leaving especially the children, "the lambs of this flock," untended. He warns against contention at home and Arminianism close by, and he advises them "to see to it" that his replacement is a man of "sound principles" and "fervent piety" to stay "the torrent of error, and prejudice" of the times. He prays for them and asks their prayers, "whatever opinion" they hold about communion. "And," he ends, "let us all remember, and never forget our future solemn meeting on that great day of the Lord; the day of infallible decision, and of the everlasting and unalterable sentence."[47] To a friend a few days later he writes at length of the "evil time in Northampton" and then adds, "My youngest child but one has long been in a very infirm, afflicted and decaying, state with the rickets, and some other disorders. I desire your prayers for it."[48] Thus publicly and privately Edwards put a close to more than twenty-three years among his people. They for their part voted once again in November to be shut of him: they refused to let him preach to them though they had yet to find a pastor to take his place.[49]

As word of his dismissal spread, he received offers of settlement from churches here and abroad. Impoverished, though friends in Scotland had "generously contributed a handsome sum," and burdened by "a numerous and chargeable family," Edwards at forty-seven accepted a call in December to become missionary to over two hundred Housatonics and minister to a dozen settlers in the outpost village of Stockbridge, Massachusetts, some fifty miles west of Northampton. Even so, rumors persisted that he would found another church in town. To still such talk and the "great tumult" that ensued, on 19 May a second council advised Edwards that "he should leave Northampton, and accept of the mission to which he was invited at Stockbridge."[50] The formal end to the affair came three years later.

In a letter, now lost, of 11 August 1754, Joseph Hawley wrote to Edwards, apologizing for his part in his dismissal, confessing his sins and his errors, seeking forgiveness, desiring judgment. Edwards agrees to the last, reluctantly: "it obliges me renewedly to resolve in my mind, and particularly to look over, that most disagreeable and dreadful scene, the Particulars of which I have long since dismiss'd from my mind, as having no Pleasure in the Thoughts of them." It hurts so much to remember: "So deep were their Prejudices, that their Heat was maintained, nothing would quiet 'em till they could see the Town clear of Root & Branch, Name and Remnant." It would take "no less than a quire of Paper" to record the offending details, to limn the "unreasonable violent spirit" that attended committees and councils. Rather than check such intemperateness, Hawley encouraged it, forsaking kinship, "confident, magisterial, vehement," a man not only "uncharitable and censorious" but capable of "bold slanders asserted in strong Terms & delivered in very severe opprobrious Language." A leader in such affairs "may expect to be distinguished by God's Frowns," unless he leads the people to repentance as he led them to transgression. But Edwards wearies of the task Hawley has put upon him, and he leaves his judgment with the younger man, a judgment, he adds, unalterable "as long as I live." He has had quite enough. "One thing I must desire of you, & that is, that if you dislike what I have written, you would not expect that I should carry on any Paper or Letter Controversy with you on the subject. I have had enough of this Controversy, and desire to have done with it. I have spent enough of the precious Time of my Life in it heretofore. I desire and pray that God may enable you to view things truly, & as he views them; and so to act in the affair as shall be best for you, & most for your Peace living & dying."[51] And so he leaves a suppliant Hawley, as earlier he had left an unrepentant congregation, to a just and, as Edwards hints, a vengeful God. For himself he wanted nothing but the time and the peace of his study. At first he had neither in Stockbridge.

Theologian in Exile

Politics and the life of the mind.   Installed there on 8 August 1751, he quickly got caught up in village politics and the competing demands of the London Society for the Propagation of the Gospel in New England, the Boston Commissioners to Indian Affairs, and, again, the Williams clan of bitter memory. It was a Williams—Solomon of Lebanon, Connecticut—who in 1751 finally published the doctrinal justification for his dismissal, an argument Edwards felt compelled to answer. *Misrepresentations Corrected* (1752) is a scrupulous and devastating attack on Williams and "the true absurdity" of the scheme. After a hundred pages of citations and polemic, Edwards pauses momentarily—"Perhaps instances enough of this have already been taken notice of; yet I would now mention some others"—and then plunges ahead for seventy more pages.[52] And it was another Williams—Ephraim—one of the founders of the Stockbridge mission and an opponent of his settlement there, who later thwarted Edwards's efforts on behalf of the Indians and their boarding schools. After years of contention and the "unsuccessful intrigue and disappointed avarice" of the Williamses (and the Dwights), the Boston Commissioners agreed with Edwards to remove Ephraim from the conduct of their affairs.[53] But the prospects for hope ended with a fresh outbreak of war between the French and English in 1754, and peace among the Housatonics and Mohawks was the first casualty.

Still, as he wrote his father, his family liked Stockbridge "far better than they expected" and the Indians seemed "much pleased" with Sarah. Their reaction to him was mixed: though his pastoral care won over many of them, his pulpit English put them off, for he knew little of their tongue and they little of his. Most important of all to him, though, was his distance from the rancor of the past: "Here, at present, we live in peace; which has of long time been an unusual thing with us."[54] And in time, despite village squabbles and fits of the ague, he preached elsewhere[55] and finished an important study he had put aside for the Northampton troubles. "I had made considerable preparation, and was deeply engaged in the prosecution" of the case against Arminianism, he wrote to John Erskine three days after his farewell sermon, "before I was rent off from it by these difficulties."[56] Two years later, again to Erskine, he speaks of his intention to write about "*Freewill and Moral Agency*" and the "palpable inconsistency and absurdity" of the Arminian argument.[57] By 14 April 1753, he can report to Erskine that he has "almost finished the first draught."[58] In early 1754, Samuel Kneeland of Boston brought out *Freedom of the Will*, the most sustained and withering assault ever mounted against the notion of free will and, fittingly, the last of his things Edwards saw in print.

Princeton.   By the middle of July he was felled by "the longest and most tedious sickness" of his life; it lasted six months and left him, by his own account, "exceedingly wasted," very much "like a skeleton," unable to write even personal letters. That and a "great disturbance among the Indians"[59] broke in upon other work he had in mind and under pen, a companion piece on original sin that was well along, another on virtue and beauty, a third on the end of creation, a fourth on special and common grace—all of them critical aspects of his abiding faith in divine sovereignty. He sifted through his miscellanies to recover other promises he had made to himself years ago, to write a *summa theologica,* "A Rational Account of the Main Doctrines of the Christian Religion Attempted."

He never got to do it, for on 24 September 1757, Aaron Burr, his son-in-law and second president of the College of New Jersey (Princeton), died, and the trustees, meeting five days later, named Edwards to succeed him. As he wrote them on 19 October, he was "not a little surprised, on receiving the unexpected notice." Reluctant to leave Stockbridge, just as the family "scarcely got over the trouble and damage sustained by [their] removal from Northampton," Edwards pleaded that he was ill-suited to teach the young: frail health, he argued, affected his "speech, presence, and demeanor," and deficiencies "in some parts of learning," his qualifications. Mainly, though, taking on a new task would keep him from old ones, studies that "swallowed up" his mind, that were "the chief entertainment and delight" of his life. Among them were a study of "controverted points" between Arminians and Calvinists other than those already expressed in *Freedom of the Will*; a *History of the Work of Redemption,* "a Body of Divinity in an entire new method"; *The Harmony of the Old and New Testament,* a "great work" of three parts on prophecies, types, and doctrines; and "many other things in hand" in one stage of preparation or another. "So far as I myself am able to judge what talents I have, for benefiting my fellow creatures by word, I think I can write better than I can speak." Yet though his "heart is so much in these studies," he is just as "much at a loss" where his duty lies, and so, he concludes, he will seek out the Boston Commissioners.[60] They, and a council of ministerial friends he called together, urged the Princeton offer on him. He was "uncommonly moved and affected" by their advice and "fell into tears" before them.[61] Four days later, on 8 January 1758, Edwards preached his farewell sermon to the Indians; on 16 February, the corporation of the college inducted him as presi-

dent. A week later he was inoculated against smallpox; a month later
he was dead.

A "dark parade." Edwards had gone off to Princeton in January
with his daughter Lucy, leaving the rest of the family to follow in the
spring. He was met at the college with "great satisfaction and joy,"
but shortly thereafter word came of his father's death. The new president preached "sabbath after sabbath," gave out "some questions on
divinity to the senior class," and, with his widowed daughter Esther,
her small children, and many others in Princeton, had himself inoculated to ward off the infection spreading from nearby towns. After an
initially favorable reaction to the toxin, "a secondary fever set in" and
raged on uncontrolled.[62]

"[I]t seems to me [he told Lucy] to be the Will of God that I must shortly leave you, therefore give my kindest love to my dear Wife & tell her
that the uncommon Union that has so long subsisted between us has been
of such a Nature as I trust is Spiritual, and therefore will continue for ever:
and I hope she shall be supported under so Great a trial and submit chear-
fully to the Will of God; And as to my Children you are now like to be
left Fatherless which I hope will be an Inducement to you all to seek a
Father who will never fail you; & as to my Funeral I would have it to be
like unto Mr Burrs, and any additional sum of Money that might be expected to be laid out that way, I would have it disposed of to charitable
uses."[63]

He died, Dr. William Shippen recalled,[64] in "cheerful resignation" and
with "perfect freedom from pain" on 22 March 1758: he was fifty-four.
"What shall I say!," wrote his wife to their daughter Susannah. "A
holy and good God has covered us with a dark cloud. O that we may
kiss the rod, and lay our hands on our mouths! The Lord has done it.
He had made me adore his goodness, that we had him so long. But
God lives; and he has my heart. O what a legacy my husband, and
your father, has left us! We are all given to God; and there I am, and
love to be."[65] Within four days, 7 April, her daughter Esther died,
probably from the inoculation; within six months, 2 October, Sarah
Edwards died of dysentery in Philadelphia, where she had gone to look
after her orphaned grandchildren.

Edwards left a pair of spectacles, two wigs, three black coats—two
in poor condition—and over three hundred books, twenty-two of his

own devising.[66] Seven volumes have been published since, *Original Sin* (1758) and *True Virtue* (1765) among them, as well as collections of his sermons beginning in the late eighteenth century (1780, 1788, and 1789) and collections of his work in the beginning of the nineteenth: the eight-volume Leeds edition (1806–11), the eight-volume Worcester (American) edition (1808–9), and the ten-volume New York (Converse) edition (1829–30). In 1957, Yale University began the publication of the complete works with a critical edition of *Freedom of the Will*; by 1980 the sixth volume in the series appeared, Edwards's scientific and philosophical writings. It is to those early speculations that we now turn.

Chapter Two
"Things to be Considered"

Thunder, Jonathan Edwards recalled, "uncommonly terrified" him when he was young, but after his conversion he "rejoiced" in the play of lightning and the gathering storm, in God's "majestic and awful voice" upon the darkening hills. He would "chant forth" his meditations then, and he would "speak in a singing voice."[1] About that time as well—it was the summer of 1722, when he was eighteen and preparing for his first pastorate—he began a list of "Things to be Considered and Written Fully About."[2] No. 17 of the first series touches on "the cause why thunder that is a great way off will sound very grum." Edwards saw no difficulty in this, trying to explain scientifically the awful, distant voice of God. To him and his generation, the physical world no less than the moral one was subject to God's unalterable laws, and to discover them was to learn, in a small way, of His exquisite design and to know His manifest glory.

Reason and religion, unlike the antagonists the eighteenth century saw them become, were compatible, all but identical. In another unfinished proposal, "A Rational Account of the Main Doctrines of the Christian Religion Attempted,"[3] Edwards hoped to show "how all arts and sciences, the more they are perfected, the more they issue to divinity, and coincide with it, and appear to be as parts of it." Newton, after all, ended his *Opticks* (1704)—a particularly important text for Edwards—by observing that the pursuit of science "enlarged" the sphere of moral philosophy such that "our Duty towards [God], as well as towards one another, will appear to us by the Light of Nature."[4] Like Newton, Edwards keeps God in conclusion. He defers to the penultimate paragraph of his remarks on sea-bound flying spiders his admiration for "the wisdom of the Creator . . . [in] annually carrying off and burying the corruption and nauseousness of our air . . . in the bottom of the ocean where it will do no harm."[5] Still, Edwards's science differs markedly from Newton's.

With rare exception, his is a deductive exercise verified by logic, not by experiment, and he speculates about natural events using little empirical data. For example, he accounts for successive claps of thunder that reverberate from a single lightning bolt by noting that "the lightning is incredibly swifter than the sound. These things are so far certain and demonstrable that it is impossible that it should happen otherwise."[6] The smell of the lamp clings to such science and, in fact, a good deal of what Edwards "proves" can be traced to theories and demonstrations in the standard texts then used at Yale. Though he resolved to be "impartial" to new discoveries and to "receive them if rational" however long he had followed "another way,"[7] he had earlier accepted divine sovereignty and the order and harmony it implied. That meant, for Edwards, not a limited but a complementary world, one of corresponding truths, in which proportion, for instance, imparted beauty in nature and virtue in man. In a coherent world of divine sovereignty, ideas of virtue and ideas of beauty—ethics and aesthetics—were simply different expressions of the same thing. Or, as a commonplace of the time put it, the book of nature opened the book of God. Edwards read both carefully. "Lightning more commonly strikes high things," he wrote at the close of the decade, "such as high towers, spires, and pinnacles, and high trees, and is observed to be more terrible in mountainous places, which may signifie that heaven is an enemy to all proud persons and that [God] especially makes the marks of his vengeance, Isa. 2.12–15."[8]

In time Edwards gave up his science, but he held to his delight in the natural world, bred in his boyhood years along the banks of the Connecticut River and renewed day after day in solitary rambles through the woods of Northampton and the wilderness of Stockbridge. Whatever made him turn to other matters—the example of his father, his self-confessed difficulty with mathematics, his lack of recognition, his pastoral duties—he always kept alive his sense of place and his interest in the conduct of natural affairs. Thunder and lightning both terrified and taught him. That was the wonder of the world.

Studies in Natural Philosophy

Flying spiders and the benefits of modesty. Edwards's earliest scientific work was probably composed during his senior year at Yale. "Of Insects" is an illustrated text written on both sides of a folio page describing the ways of the flying or ballooning spider.[9] This "wonderful" creature suspends itself from a web fastened to a tree and then produces another, finer web, which is carried aloft by currents of air

and "by the spider's permission" until, touching another tree, it becomes fastened there. The spider marches—flies—across a space determined by the length of the web, the weight of the spider, and the force
of the wind. Edwards solves "the whole mystery" of the spider's flight
by repeated trials. He holds a very large spider against a dark background to examine how it spins so fine a thread; again and again, he
breaks a connecting filament with a stick to induce the spider to weave
another. And he reminisces: "I remember that, when I was a boy, I
have at the same time of year lien on the ground upon my back and
beheld abundances of them, all flying southeast, which I then thought
were going to a warm country."

On 31 October 1723, just after he turned twenty, Edwards recorded
his findings in a letter to Judge Paul Dudley, one of his father's correspondents and a colonial fellow of the Royal Society of London.[10]
Except for a sprinkling of "Sir's" and a somewhat more elaborate chart
of illustrations, Edwards's first "published" work reproduces the earlier
text in detail and closes upon a young man's hope of recognition,
though chary of his success. "I humbly beg to be pardoned for running
the venture, though an utter stranger, of troubling you with so prolix
an account of that which I am altogether uncertain whether you will
esteem worthy of the time and pains of reading. Pardon me if I thought
it might at least give you occasion to make better observations of these
wondrous animals, that should be worthy of communicating to the
learned world, from whose glistening webs so much of the wisdom of
the Creator shines." There is no record of a reply, nor, for all his defer-
ence, is there mention of Edwards in the papers of the Royal Society.[11]
But in 1832 the learned world he had sought came to know his work
on flying spiders and to praise it. Benjamin Silliman concluded that
had Edwards devoted himself to science he might have been "another
Newton."[12] Coming from the most influential scientist in early nineteenth-century America that was high praise indeed. It was also a
hundred years too late.

The studied humility that closes the letter to Judge Dudley finds its
way onto the coverleaf of a collection of notes and fragmentary essays
Edwards would later call "Natural Philosophy," the usual name for
science in the eighteenth century. There, on the coverleaf, in remarks
written at about the time of the letter and often in shorthand, Edwards
recites the benefits of modesty, a beginning writer's advice to himself.
"The world will expect more modesty because of my circumstances—
in America, young, etc. Let there be a superabundance of modesty, and

though perhaps 'twill otherwise be needless, it will wonderfully make way for its reception in the world. Mankind are by nature proud and exceeding envious, and ever jealous of such upstarts; and it exceedingly irritates and affronts 'em to see 'em appear in print. Yet the modesty ought not to be affected and foolish, but decent and natural." He will strive, he adds several months later, for order, clarity, and artlessness— "Let it not look as if I was much read, or conversant with books or the learned world"—and for a plain style "so that the ideas shall be left naked."[13]

Prejudices and fragments. Just inside the coverleaf, put there probably by a later editor, stands a "Lemma to the whole," Edwards's plea for an open mind or at least a mind free of a limiting past. "Of Prejudices of the Imagination"[14] recognizes the unhappy prospects for change because "opinions arising from imagination take us as soon as we are born, are beat into us by every act of sensation," grow with us, and become the very structure of our minds. Contrary ideas strike us as "dissonant." In time what we "actually perceive by [our] senses" we make "the standard of possibility and impossibility." To "remedy" this prejudice, Edwards considers at length two theorems—one on the velocity of bodies, the other on their size—and shows how unexamined notions about the natural world distort truths about it. Of course, he fails to "put every man clean out of conceit with his imagination," notwithstanding nine figures and seven postulata. But the paper typifies, more nearly than does "Of Insects," his method of scientific inquiry through diagram and deduction.

"Natural Philosophy" gathers together ideas of a dozen years or so, roughly from his graduate years at Yale through the early years of his Northampton settlement, but few of the 133 articles get "written fully about" as he had once planned: problems of refraction, binocularism, and color; of circulation, respiration, and musculature; of spheroids, fixed stars, and comets; of gravity, density, and elasticity; of mountains, twigs, and bubbles; of ice and "the saltness of the sea."[15] Not bound in the manuscript but written at the same time and related to it are four more papers, brief and tentative.[16] In one, Edwards attempts a "full account" of the rainbow, with some help from Descartes and Newton, but he abandons the single folio page in midsentence. In "Of Light Rays," he computes the thickness of a ray of starlight to twenty-three places, concluding that in some instances it may be "less than any man will have patience to make figures for." In "Beauty of the World," he speaks of the "sweet mutual consents" of the natural world within itself and with God, how the "gentle motions of the trees, of lily, etc. . . . represent calmness, gentleness, benevolence, etc.," but he puts off to another time more extended correspondences. In yet another paper, "Wisdom in the Contrivance of the World," he proposes to number God's remarkable and purposeful designs in nature, but he ends the catalogue at five. Still, two papers included in "Natural Philosophy" are developed sufficiently to catch the argument of divine sovereignty at the center of Edwards's thought, and the first and longer of them, "Of Atoms,"[17] probes the immateriality of the world. It also blurs the categories of science and philosophy and theology.[18]

The structure of matter.   Atoms are indivisible—"indiscerpible" is Edwards's word—or perfect bodies, held together in themselves and to one another by an infinite power. That God alone exercises such infinite power makes the very nature of the atom "an incontestable argument for the being of God." And just as that infinite power keeps bodies in being, so it had first to bring them into being: God "created and preserves the world." Mechanistic explanations—Newton's laws of motion, for example, or gravity—report partially if they do not acknowledge God's being and the immediate and continued exercise of His infinite power, for it is clear that bodies exist only as God wills them to be. Without God there is nothing. "So that the substance of bodies at last becomes either nothing, or nothing but the Deity acting in that particular manner in those parts of space where he thinks fit. So that, speaking most strictly, there is no proper substance but God himself." So, strictly speaking, there is no matter. Later, in its "proper place," Edwards planned to prove that matter is not substance, to refute Thomas Hobbes (and Descartes and Newton) and put an end to materialism, dualism, and mechanism.[19] But now, in "Of Atoms," he abides a material world in order to explain it. "And let the force that [the perfect body] e is to withstand be as great as you please—if the weight of the universe falling against it from never so great a distance, and as much more as you please—we can prove, and what is said above does prove, that it would neither bend nor break, but stiffly bear the shock of it all." Further on, Edwards equates body with solidity and both with "indefinite resistance." Whatever he called it, and he preferred the last, it depends for its being upon God's infinite power.

"Of Being,"[20] a later paper, takes up the question of matter immediately and starkly, "That there should absolutely be nothing at all is utterly impossible." The mind cannot conceive "a perfect nothing" (as it can a perfect solid), nor can words express nothing "without speaking horrid nonsense." It is necessary that some thing be eternal, infinite, and omnipresent. Space is, Edwards concludes, and so is God. "I had as good speak plain: I have already said as much as that space is God." Is it possible, Edwards then asks, "that anything should be, and nothing know it?" No, "because nothing has any existence anywhere else but in consciousness. No, certainly nowhere else, but either in created or uncreated consciousness." Nothing can be without being known. Suppose, for instance, that the world were deprived of the properties of solids, of shapes and colors, of size and motion, of matter itself. "There would be neither white nor black, neither blue nor brown, bright nor shaded, pellucid nor opaque; no noise or sound, neither heat nor cold, neither fluid nor wet nor dry, hard or soft, nor solidity, nor extension nor figure, nor magnitude, nor proportions; nor body, nor spirit. What then is become of the universe? Certainly, it exists nowhere but in the divine mind." To think that material things are substantial or that spirits are shadows is "a gross mistake." The contrary is true. Matter is not substance. Being exists in the mind, "either infinite or finite," in consciousness and in knowledge. God is the only substance, mind the only reality.

Speculations on the Mind

Excellency and the ideal world.   Edwards explores the problem of the mind further in his most sustained piece of philosophical thought from these years, a manuscript collection of about sixty items—he added a dozen more by 1747—that he later entitled "The Natural History of the Mental World." The original plan for "The Mind"[21] calls for an introduction "Concerning the two worlds, the external and the internal: the external, the subject of natural philosophy; the internal, our own minds. How the knowledge of the latter is in many respects the most important. Of what great use the true knowledge of this is, and of what dangerous consequence errors here are, more than in the other." He sketches out fifty-six "subjects to be handled": prejudice, vanity, certainty, affections, appetite, will, "the sense of the heart," liberty, blame, beauty, perception, love; how "the mind would be without ideas except as suggested by the senses"; how "ideas or thoughts and judgments may be said to be innate." But he never gets to many of them, turning instead to some subjects time and time again, to excellency, the first and longest article in the reconstructed text, no fewer than seven times, to existence five times, to substance

three. With the second entry, "Place of Minds," he embarks on a tide
of commentaries on John Locke's *An Essay Concerning Human Understanding* (1690). Many of the entries of "The Mind" shuttle between
those in the "Miscellanies," a scrapbook of ideas Edwards began during
his New York pastorate.[22]

Excellency is "the consent of being to being, or being's consent to
entity"; the more consent or agreement there is or the more being there
is, the greater the excellency. Beauty comes from this, pleasure, holiness, and love, and all are based upon a perception of similarity, upon
what Edwards calls an "identity of relation." Simple beauty, for example, consists of a single relation, equality; complex beauty consists
of a complex relation, proportion; and, since matter is "but the shadow
of being," the greatest beauty consists of the consent of spirit to spirit.
No beauty—or pleasure or holiness or love, as far as that goes—exists
in oneness, for being consents to being mutually. And infinite beauty
is the "infinite consent of being in general," in other words, the Trinity, the infinite mutual love of the Father and the Son, which love
itself is the Holy Spirit. Thus all creation is "resolved into love," and
we consent to nature's law and to God's in the "sweet harmony" of a
necessary relation. Ours is a coherent world, joined and sensible.

And it is an ideal one, an image in the mind of God. Edwards
implied as much in "Of Atoms" and "Of Being"; now, in "The Mind,"
he makes his argument clearer still, and he begins it with the ways we
see. "The idea we have of space, and what we call by that name, is
only colored space." Take color away and space is gone; we see nothing.
Color itself, all natural philosophers agree, is in the mind, not in the
thing; it is an idea, "and nothing like it can be out of the mind." But
for the blind there is no color, in the mind or out; no motion either,
no extension, figure, distance, or space; no matter, except what can be
realized imperfectly, a vague sense of things, hardly more than "the
pain we have by the scratch of a pin." For the sighted the case is much
the same: we are sand-blind. What we call a thing, what we mean or
intend by the name we give it, vaguely renders the idea we have of it
in our minds. Thus nothing exists out of the mind quite as it does in
the mind or as it does "in some other mind or minds," in the like-
minded, for instance, or in the divine mind.

And indeed, the secret lies here: that which truly is the substance of all bodies
is the infinitely exact and precise and perfectly stable idea in God's mind,
together with his stable will that the same shall gradually be communicated

to us, and to other minds, according to certain fixed and exact established methods and laws: or in somewhat different language, the infinitely exact and precise divine idea, together with an answerable, perfectly exact, precise and stable will with respect to correspondent communications to created minds, and effects on their minds.

God makes known the physical world through fixed laws over time, gradually, and in different ways to different minds. He creates—conceives—matter moment by moment throughout time in the exercise of His will and through the power of His mind. In short, the substance of all matter is an idea in the mind of God.

Once more: if color does not exist out of the mind, nor motion, extension, figure, distance, nor space, then nothing exists out of the mind except, perhaps, resistance. Still, if nothing is resisted, then there is no resistance, only the power of resistance and God's "constant law or method" governing it. And if resistance is really out of the mind, one law of resistance must resist another law of resistance, a patent absurdity. If, on the other hand, resistance exists in the mind "as a mode of an idea," then an idea of, say, color may be resisted. "The world is therefore an ideal one; and the law of creating, and the succession of these ideas, is constant and regular."

The reality of God.   Even so, we still speak "in the old way." Although the material world exists nowhere but in the mind—an idea itself, for the mind exists only "mentally"—we assume a real world in order to comment upon it. Obviously, our imperfect notions of the world cannot answer God's perfect idea of it. Had we a perfect idea of the present, we would have a perfect idea of the past, because the present includes the successive revelations of the past, and we would then know as well the purpose of each revelation and the end of all of them. In fact, we know the present (and the world) only imperfectly, know it, "as is vulgarly thought," materially, and know its meaning and its design but dimly. Yet the physical world adumbrates the spiritual—an old truth—and though we see it imperfectly, it is all we know and all we need to know. "For the corporeal world is to no advantage but to the spiritual, and it is exactly the same advantage this way as the other; for it is all one as to anything excited in the mind."

The physical world is a fixed series of ideas that God excites in created minds such that "God and real existence are the same." But, Edwards asks, what is "real" existence, what of things no created mind sees, what of things, for instance, in a room closed to our view? They exist, he answers, as part of a series of things "supposed" by God according to "his own settled order," and they constitute an integral system. God acts "as if they, the things supposed, were in actual idea." Thus Edwards solves (for himself) the nagging problem of real existence in an ideal world: things are real because God in the wholeness of His mind supposes them to be so. That created minds may not be aware of them simply illustrates once again the limitations of imperfect minds.

Experience and innate knowledge.   Differences in experience just compound the problem. Suppose God were to create another Edwards "in some distant part of the universe," endow him with the same ideas and the same memory, but then set in motion "a different train of ideas" as he came to exist. The two Edwardses would not be the same: their experiences would differ, and their compassion. "Will anyone say that he, in such a case, is the same person with me," Edwards asks in the closing lines of "The Mind," "when I know nothing of his sufferings and am never the better for his joys?" And because experiences differ so radically form one person to another, he adds, we can know the workings of only our own minds, not another's. All we can hope for then is a relation of minds, in excellency, in the consent of being to being, a harmony that, among other things, warrants the separateness of minds while forging links of affection between them.

Experience alters perception and, as Edwards recalls, often corrects it. "I can remember when I was so young, that seeing two things in the same building, one of which was twice so far off as the other, yet seeing one over the other, I thought they had been of the same distance, one right over the other. My senses then were deceitful in that thing, though they made the same representations as now; and yet now they are not deceitful. The only difference is in experience." Earlier, he had pointed to yet another cause of changed perceptions, the state of being. We perceive by one rule when the mind and body are united, by another "no doubt" when they no longer are. In the first state, we "passively receive" ideas communicated by God "immediately"; in the second state, we perceive by some yet unknown rule.

But this much is clear: the mind is not just passive, it is also "abundantly active." The mind contemplates, reflects, abstracts, is "active about its own ideas." And it is intuitive. Take the matter of simple causation: though we usually reason from cause and design, finding order and sequence and regularity in a bounty of particulars, there are

some things, like existence and the consciousness of it, that we know
not from discernible cause but from intuition. We know intuitively
what is so exquisitely rational, that cause is sequential, or, as Edwards puts it, "Cause is that, after or upon the existence of which,
or the existence of it after such a manner, the existence of another
thing follows." We know intuitively that uncaused existence is a
contradiction, that when anything begins to be, there must be an
antecedent cause. "This is an innate principle, in the sense that the
soul is born with it, a necessary fatal propensity so to conclude on
every occasion." Any new existence, any alteration in existence has a
cause. That is true of the material world no less than the immaterial,
of a solid accelerating from rest no less than a spirit inclining toward
holiness.

For instance, if there had been nothing but one globe of solid matter, which
in time past had been at perfect rest, if it starts away into motion, we conclude
there is some cause of that alteration; or if that globe in time past had been
moving in a straight line, and turns short about at right angles with its former
direction; or if it have been moving with such a degree of celerity, and all at
once moves with but half that swiftness. And it is all one whether these
alterations be in body or in spirits, their beginning must have a cause—the
first alteration that there is in a spirit after it is created, let it be an alteration
in what it will, and so the rest. So if a spirit always in times past had had
such an inclination, for instance, always loved and chosen sin, and then has a
quite contrary inclination and loves and chooses holiness, the beginning of
this alteration, or the first new existence in that spirit towards it, whether it
were some action or whatsoever, had some cause.[23]

Edwards borrows from Newton and simply stretches the first and second laws of motion to fit a moral world. But the argument on causality
also reveals that he departed from the other principal source of his
scientific and philosophical thought, John Locke.[24]

Edwards on Locke. According to his contemporary biographer,
Edwards read Locke for the first time like "the most greedy miser in
gathering handfuls of silver and gold from some new discovered treasure."[25] By the time he composed the article on causal reasoning, No.
54—it follows the one on the fallibility of the senses—apparently some
of the glitter was gone. He had, of course, borrowed his psychology
from Locke: that an idea is an object of the mind; that ideas are simple,
complex, and abstract; that simple ideas derive from the senses; that
all ideas come from either sensation or reflection. But at the same time,

he held that certain ideas, like causality, are innate and certain knowledge immediate. In positing that, Edwards rejects the basic tenet and
metaphor of Locke's *Essay*: the mind at first is "white Paper" upon
which the senses tally experience. And, Locke added, though the operations of the mind, such as its ability to think or to doubt, may be
innate, its ideas are not.[26]

Edwards disagreed. "Things," he remarks in No. 19, "that we know
by immediate sensation, we know intuitively, as they are properly self-
evident truths: as, grass is green, the sun shines, honey is sweet." He
disagreed on other important points as well, on the question of personal identity, for one (No. 11): "Well might Mr. Locke say that identity of person consisted in identity of consciousness; for he might have
said that identity of spirit, too, consisted in the same consciousness."
And he continued to question Locke later on as well. Sometime about
1747, for instance, when he was thinking of a treatise on the will, he
wrote (No. 70), "That it is not uneasiness in our present circumstances
that always determines the will, as Mr. Locke supposes, is evident by
this: that there may be an act of the will in choosing and determining
to forbear to act or move when some other action is proposed to a man,
as well as in choosing to act."[27] Yet for all the differences between them
over the years, Locke profoundly affected the young man starting out,
and traces of empiricism are not hard to find in his published work,
early, in *A Divine and Supernatural Light* (1734), and late, in *Religious
Affections* (1746).[28]

But Edwards was not only thinking through Locke (and Newton)
at Yale. He was also foraging in the Bible, keeping "Notes on Scripture" as well as notes on "The Mind," calculating both the number
of the beast for "Notes on the Apocalypse" and the distance of fixed
stars for "Of Light Rays."[29] During his New York sojourn, he had
resolved "To study the Scriptures so steadily, constantly and frequently, as that I may find, and plainly perceive myself to grow in
the knowledge of the same."[30] Shortly after, he recorded the first
notes in a catalogue of biblical types in nature, "Images or Shadows of Divine Things." By the end of the decade, he began to
interleave the family Bible with "miscellaneous observations" and
textual explications that in time grew to over nine hundred manuscript
pages.[31]

A year or two before starting the "Blank Bible," Edwards wrote a
one-page outline of "A Rational Account of the Main Doctrines of the
Christian Religion." Like so many other projects he attempted in the

'twenties, he never quite brought it off. Still, the title describes, as perhaps no other words can, the thoughtful work of a life-time, Edwards's attempt to create a rational account of the main doctrines of the Christian religion.

Chapter Three

Scriptural and Rational Doctrines

"In short," added Thomas Prince and William Cooper in their preface, the "noble" subject Jonathan Edwards pitched upon with such "strength and clearness" for his Boston public lecture on 8 July 1731, was "the very soul of piety." *God Glorified in the Work of Redemption By the Greatness of Man's Dependence on Him, in the Whole of it* (1731) was published, as the title page went on to say, "at the Desire of several Ministers and Others, in Boston, who heard it," a small octavo volume of twenty-five pages.[1] It was, Prince and Cooper thought, surety that the "evangelical principles" of Solomon Stoddard would "shine" in his grandson and proof, despite his twenty-seven years, that Edwards was a "workman" the equal of his gospel brethren. They hoped—it came to a little more than that—that Yale (and Harvard) would be "a fruitful mother of many such sons." Ten years later, at the onset of the Great Awakening, Cooper wrote a long preface to *Distinguishing Marks* (1741), recommending Edwards's apologia for the revival, "strongly drawn from scripture, reason, and experience"[2]; and later still, a year before Edwards's dismissal, Prince (and three others) wrote in praise of his *Humble Inquiry* (1749), a scriptural defense of traditional communion practice.[3] The Boston ministers, that early summer's day, heard better than they knew.

And what they heard was the old orthodoxy. At the close of the decade Edwards turned to the work of redemption once again, this time in a series of sermons for his Northampton congregation, put together, he told the Princeton College trustees many years later, "in an entire new method."[4] Yet that notion—an old orthodoxy in a new method—characterizes more than *A History of the Work of Redemption,* more than the sermons and the narratives of the 1730s. It stamps as well the works of the 1740s and the 1750s and, of course, the mind that conceived them. Edwards's assumptions were founded on doctrinal orthodoxy—on divine sovereignty and original sin and free grace—

34

freshened by contemporary philosophical thought from abroad, challenged by the realities of a New England parish nearing mid-century,
and submitted to a logic unremitting and unforgiving. He wrote and
published, as thoroughly as long hours and a shortened life would allow, a rational and inventive account, a strict and lively orthodoxy.[5]

The Sovereignty of God

God Glorified and the triadic form. The "strength and clearness" Prince and Cooper attributed to Edwards owed much to the
structure he used to frame his argument, the three-part form of the
sermon familiar to generations of Puritans and the form he always
used.[6] Typically, a minister "opened" a biblical text, explored the doctrine it implied, and urged its application or practical uses upon his
congregation: explication, exposition, and exhortation; word, idea,
and experience. The text for *God Glorified* is 1 Cor. 1:29–31: "That no
flesh should glory in his presence. But of him are ye in Christ Jesus,
who of God is made unto us wisdom, and righteousness, and sanctification, and redemption: That, according as it is written, He that glo-
rieth, let him glory in the Lord." Edwards locates these verses in the
immediate context of the epistle—the wisdom of the "learned Gre-
cians"—and then closes in on the words themselves. "*He is made of God
unto us wisdom*: In him are all the proper good and true excellency of
the understanding. Wisdom was a thing that the Greeks admired; but
Christ is the true light of the world; it is through him that true wisdom
is imparted to the mind." The doctrine then pointedly restates the text:
"'God is glorified in the work of redemption in this, that there appears
in it so absolute and universal a dependence of the redeemed on him.'"

Commentary on the doctrine underscores its subject in a triad of
prepositions increasingly internal. All good comes of God, through
God, in God, all grace and all power, of the Father, through the Son,
in the Holy Ghost. "That they [the redeemed] have all their good of
him, and that they have all through him, and that they have all in
him: That he be the cause and original whence all their good comes,
therein it is *of* him; and that he is the medium by which it is obtained
and conveyed, therein they have it *through* him; and that he is good
itself given and conveyed, therein it is *in* him." As from a distance,
the redeemed come closer and closer to God in the successive work of
the trinity. Edwards exhorts his hearers to reject any scheme of divinity
"inconsistent with our entire dependence on God for all" and to "exalt

God alone; as by trust and reliance, so by praise," a triad once more. As absolute sovereign, God exacts tribute and grants favor, indeed, life itself, much as fabled eastern kings might. Man is nothing, "wholly defiled" and "infinitely odious," "naked and wholly without any good." His dependence upon God is absolute; his need for the trinity, complete.

Biblical quotation—again, typical of both the traditional form of the sermon and Edwards's practice—stirs and thickens the argument. In three consecutive paragraphs on the inherent good of God, Edwards cites the New Testament fourteen times; in the next paragraph, the last in the section on man's dependence on God for all his good, he uses two scriptural passages, the second explaining the first.[7] Sometimes a biblical phrase leads him to metaphors of his own. In the first of the four paragraphs, he expands upon Heb. 2:10 and man's holiness: "The saints are beautiful and blessed by a communication of God's holiness and joy, as the moon and planets are bright by the sun's light." Earlier, Edwards turned the suggestion of 1 Pet. 1:15 on God's power of grace into another natural figure: "As grace is at first from God, so it is continually from him, and is maintained by him, as much as light in the atmosphere is all day long from the sun, as well as at first dawning, or at sunrising."[8]

Images of man's dependence.   But usually Edwards fixes upon a controlling image to develop his argument, as here, in *God Glorified,* an image of the marketplace.[9] Dependence for redemption in Christ— itself an implied exchange of good(s)—becomes explicitly economic: "Our blessings are what we have by purchase; and the purchase is made by God, the blessings are purchased of him, and God gives the purchaser; and not only so, but God is the purchaser. Yea God is both the purchaser and the price; for Christ, who is God, purchased these blessings for us, by offering up himself as the price of our salvation." Or the dependence becomes that of a child, the little child of Mark 10:15, as in this from the final paragraph of the sermon: "Hath any man hope that he is converted, and sanctified, and that his mind is endowed with true excellency and spiritual beauty, and his sins forgiven, and he received into God's favor, and exalted to the honor and blessedness of being his child, and an heir of eternal life; let him give God all the glory."

In casting *God Glorified* in figures of a child, of the marketplace, and of the sun, Edwards betrays something of his attitude toward traditional notions of divine sovereignty. He reads "absolute dependence" not only as the necessary human consequence of absolute divine power, but, significantly, as an expression of a child's natural need for care and love. A child stands in humility—"a great ingredient of true faith," Edwards notes in the third of four uses—and in need of the love of his parents, seeking it through them, receiving it in them, a triadic quest. Absolute dependence means "entire" dependence, or dependence upon the trinity; schemes of divinity that fail to acknowledge each of the three persons of the trinity "derogate" God and "thwart" His design. "All is of the Father, all through the Son, and all in the Holy Ghost. Thus God appears in the work of redemption as all in all." Or, to take the image of the marketplace, the business of eternal life must be a three-part transaction, for it is offered of the Father, bought through the Son, and accounted in the Holy Ghost, both price and purchaser. Lastly, the sun, as Edwards uses it here, records a vaster dependence still, though no less trinitarian. The world (of man) flows with the light of redeeming grace from the first dawning of day and gathers, through the darkness, the reflected light of the moon and the distant planets, a three-fold glory.

Whether Edwards submitted such a traditional doctrine to the Boston ministers as an earnest of his orthodoxy—a young man's word to his elders—or as an early warning to the liberal thinkers scattered among them makes little difference. He spoke out of deep conviction and he never altered his belief, never tired of explaining divine sovereignty and what it entailed, man's dependence, God's glory, the holy trinity.[10] "So much as the dependence of the creature is on God, so much greater does the creature's emptiness in himself appear; and so much the greater the creature's emptiness, so much the greater must the fulness of the Being be who supplies him. Our having all of God shews the fulness of his power and grace. Our having all through him shews the fulness of his merit and worthiness; and our having all in him demonstrates his fulness of beauty, love, and happiness." Like his words on first seeing Sarah Pierrepont or, later, in recollecting his conversion experience, these evoke the sweet sense of things. Divine sovereignty was a vital doctrine and, he knew, a comely one.

Early sermons and other orthodoxies. *God Glorified* was a revision of an earlier Northampton sermon, the substantive changes made, perhaps, with intellectual Boston in mind.[11] Like other New England ministers on a schedule of Sunday sermons and Thursday lectures (often hours long), ordinations and funerals, elections and musters, fast days and days of thanksgiving, Edwards kept a file of his sermons, revising and repeating them, usually when he was invited to preach elsewhere, particularly after he took up his labors in Stockbridge. In a quarter of a century of preaching, his file swelled to 1200 sermons or so and included assorted notebooks with subject indexes, cross-references, and dates of delivery. Though most of the sermons remain in manuscript, a few were published separately during his lifetime, more in collections after his death. Altogether not more than fifty titles were published, most the work of the 1720s and 1730s, New York and Northampton.[12]

Just to glance at the titles of several early sermons (and their texts) is to see the old orthodoxies: "The Warnings of Scripture are in the best manner adapted to the awakening and conversion of Sinners" (Luke 16:31); "Great Guilt no Obstacle to the Pardon of the returning Sinner" (Ps. 25:11); "The World judged righteously by Jesus Christ" (Acts 17:31); "The vain Self-flatteries of the Sinner" (Ps. 36:12); and "The Sin and Folly of depending on future Time" (Prov. 21:1).[13] In "The Perpetuity and Changes of the Sabbath" (1 Cor. 16:1–2), Edwards argues at some length—it runs to three sessions—that Sunday, not Saturday, is the sabbath. The Jews miscounted: they did not know "where to begin their six days, and on which particular day to rest," for in their Egyptian bondage they had "lost the true reckoning of time by the days of the week." Anyway, Edwards explains, events in the Old Testament only prefigure the New, are shadows to be interpreted: the "coming up of the children of Israel out of the Red Sea [on the sabbath], was only a type of the resurrection of Christ" on a Sunday. Besides, the Sunday sabbath is the custom in Christian countries: "Reason may greatly confirm truths revealed in the Scriptures."[14] He likens the "strange doctrine" of "The Duty of Charity to the Poor" (Deut. 15:7–12) to men who, in sowing their seed, appear to throw it away; yet they willingly "run the venture of it" and in time reap the fruits.[15] On another occasion, he sounds "A Warning to Professors of Religion" (Ezek. 23:37–39) in a language similar to that of his Enfield sermon about a decade later.

It is a wonder, that God suffers you to live upon earth; that he hath not, with a thunderbolt of his wrath, struck you down to the bottomless pit long ago. You that are allowedly and voluntarily living in sin, who have gone on hitherto in sin, are still going on, and do not design any other than to go on yet; it is a wonder that the Almighty's thunder lies still, and suffers you to sit in his house, or to live upon earth. It is a wonder that the earth will bear you, and that hell doth not swallow you up. It is a wonder that fire doth not come down from heaven, or come up from hell, and devour you; that hell-flames do not enlarge themselves to reach you, and that the bottomless pit hath not swallowed you up.[16]

In March of 1733 he balances "The Torments of the Wicked in Hell, no Occasion of Grief to the Saints in Heaven" (Rev. 10:20) with "The Wisdom of God, as display'd in the Way of Salvation by Jesus Christ, far superior to the Wisdom of Angels" (Eph. 3:10).[17] In September he traces the pilgrim's progress in one sermon and urges self-determination in four others. "To go to heaven, fully to enjoy God," Edwards tells the true Christian traveller, "is infinitely better than the most pleasant accommodations here. Better than fathers and mothers, husbands, wives or children or the company of any, or all earthly friends. These are but shadows; but the enjoyment of God is the substance. These are but scattered beams; but God is the sun. These are but streams; but God is the fountain. These are but drops; but God is the ocean."[18] He cautions his parishioners to "make use of the word as a glass wherein you may behold yourselves," tardy to church services, nodding off in lecture, silent to song, unread and unloving. "Husbands do sometimes greatly sin against God, in being of an unkind imperious behavior towards their wives, treating them as if they were servants."[19] A month before, in August, he delivered a sermon on God's free grace; it was published by Kneeland and Green in Boston early the following year "at the Desire of some the Hearers."

Free Grace and the Covenant of Faith

The divine light. *A Divine and Supernatural Light* (1734) begins where *God Glorified* ends, on the "dependence on God for means of grace," and goes on, as the running title of the sermon has it, to define "the reality of the spiritual light." The text from Matt. 16:17 strikes the pattern of definition, what is so and what is not: "And Jesus answered and said unto him, Blessed art thou, Simon Bar-jona: for flesh and blood hath not revealed it unto thee, but my Father which is in heaven." How else could "a company of poor fishermen, illiterate men" know the truth, Edwards asks, but through "God's gracious distinguishing influence and revelation"? Not only is there "such a thing as a Spiritual and Divine light," he asserts in the doctrine, it is wholly different from "any that is obtained by natural means." To prove it, he will show what it is and, first, "in a few things, what it is not."[20]

The divine light is not the conviction that natural, that is, unregenerate, men have of their sinfulness and misery. Such a conviction comes through "the light of truth," what Edwards says "may be" God's enabling gift to help men better know their fallen state, a sharp light into conscience. Though this light is not "above" nature and infuses no new principles, it is nonetheless "superior" to any that men might get by themselves and acts to check their latent wickedness. Common grace, as Edwards calls it, differs from special grace—the divine light, the divine excellency—in that it concerns the day-to-day moral world of social virtues and affections, not the spiritual world of redemption. "[S]o the Spirit of God may act upon the minds of men many ways, and communicate himself no more than when he acts upon an inanimate creature. For instance, he may excite thoughts in them, may assist their natural reason and understanding, or may assist other natural principles, and this without any union with the soul, but may act, as it were, upon an external object." Thus common grace orders the world but cannot save it.

Nor is the divine light the impressions made upon the imagination, for though the imagination may be affected by the outward beauty and glory that usually accompanies "spiritual discoveries," it may well be the changeling light of the devil. Nor is it the suggestion of "any new truths" not found in Scripture, for that may be inspiration, "such as some enthusiasts pretend to." Nor, again, is it "every affecting view" a man may have of religious matters, for that may come from "what he reads in a romance, or sees acted in a stage-play." No; the divine and supernatural light is "a real sense and apprehension of the divine excellency of things revealed in the word of God." And the "natural consequence" of this is redemption.

The sixth sense.   For Edwards, then, the divine light is a "real" sense, a "true" sense, a "sense of the heart," not of the mind, as real and as true as are the senses of natural things, of sight, sound, smell, taste, and touch, but "vastly higher," a sixth sense. It is a way of knowing akin to John Locke's empirical model in *An Essay Concerning Human Understanding,* a "new simple idea" unmediated by thought or logic, innate and a little beyond. It is the transforming light of Isaac Newton's *Opticks* made metaphor, the reconciliation of God and man in the physics of the natural world. It is the *sensus suavitatis* of John Calvin's *Institutes of the Christian Religion,* a sense or a feeling of sweetness in the promise of divine assurance, a taste of salvation.[21] It is all

these, the confluence of Edwards's philosophical, scientific, and theological thought, the new language of old belief.

A man with such a sense does not "merely rationally believe that
God is glorious, but he has a sense of the gloriousness of God in his
heart"; has not a speculative notion of God's holiness, but a "sense of
the loveliness" of it; has not the judgment that God is gracious, but a
sense of His graciousness. There is a difference between the understanding and the will (or the inclination or the heart, he adds), between
an "opinion" and a "sense." "There is a difference between having a
rational judgment that honey is sweet, and having a sense of its sweetness. A man may have the former, that knows not how honey tastes;
but a man cannot have the latter unless he has an idea of the taste of
honey in his mind. So there is a difference between believing that a
person is beautiful, and having a sense of beauty. The former may be
obtained by hearsay" (much as Edwards reports of Sarah, "They say
there is a young lady"), "but the latter only by seeing the countenance"
(such as he observes, "She will sometimes go from place to place, singing sweetly").

The true sense of the divine excellency of God's word arises both
indirectly and directly. Because the light removes prejudices from the
heart, it indirectly frees the mind to speculate, to reason with clearer
conviction. But the divine reality "commands assent" directly, and
with greater effect, because it differs so remarkably from things
"merely human." And it comes immediately of God—"A kind of intuitive and immediate evidence"—not by natural means or "any second
causes." It may make use of the natural faculties, but it is not natural;
it may lend "due apprehension" to old, scriptural truths, but it reveals
no new ones. Though there is no light without God's word, the word
does not cause the light, no more than the word of Christ's holiness,
for example, causes the sense of it. "The mind cannot see the excellency
of any doctrine, unless that doctrine be first in the mind; but seeing
the excellency of the doctrine may be immediately from the Spirit of
God; though the conveying of the doctrine, or proposition itself may
be by the word." That the divine light is both real and immediate
proves to be "abundantly" scriptural—Edwards cites sixteen texts in
less than three pages—and rational. "We cannot rationally doubt but"
that things of God are "vastly different" from things human; however,
"it is rational to suppose" that they may be seen, though not, of course,
by the sin-blind. If "it is rational to suppose" that God can communicate to man, then it is just as rational to suppose that He would

tender His best to him, His saving grace, and that He would do so "nextly from himself, and by himself, according to his own sovereign will." And if "it is rational to suppose" that the light is "beyond man's power to obtain," then it cannot belong to reason, these spiritual things of "beauty and loveliness," no more than feeling can perceive color nor sight sweetness. "Reason's work is to perceive truth and not excellency. It is not ratiocination that gives men the perception of the beauty and amiableness of a countenance, though it may be many ways indirectly an advantage to it; yet it is no more reason that immediately perceives it, than it is reason that perceives the sweetness of honey: it depends on the sense of the heart. Reason may determine that a countenance is beautiful to others, it may determine that honey is sweet to others; but it will never give me a perception of its sweetness."

The light comes to the wise and the unlearned alike, Edwards remarks in his "brief" improvements, "without a long and subtile train of reasoning." Better than the work of "the greatest philosophers or statesmen," such knowledge is "sweet and joyful," more pleasant than the study of natural, human things. It changes the soul, plumbs the heart, fires a holy and "sincere love," and convinces the faithful of "the reality of those glorious rewards that God has promised to them that obey him." Such were Edwards's closing lines that August in 1733.

Justification by faith.   Between the end of that year, a time he would later remember for the "unusual flexibleness, and yielding to advice, in our young people," and the end of the following year, when "the Spirit of God began extraordinarily to set in," he chides his flock about "The Unreasonableness of Indetermination in Religion" (1 Kings 18:21) and "The Preciousness of Time" (Eph. 5:16), urging young and old alike to choose now; he considers "Wicked Men useful in their Destruction only" (Ezek. 15:2–4); and in a thanksgiving sermon, he reproves parents for not teaching their children songs of divine praise and heavenly glory (Rev. 14:2).[22] Towards the end of 1734 he began a series of evangelical sermons on the need for salvation. Sometime later he edited a few of them and, after unaccountable delays, issued *Discourses on Various Important Subjects* (1738), the only sermon collection published during his lifetime.[23] To the four sermons selected from among several others by those at Northampton who had gained "special benefit" from them during the "remarkable season" of conversion, Edwards added a fifth, a sermon delivered in the late 1720s but one "proper" to the awakening fervor of the other four. The first of them, "Justification by Faith Alone," finds its own justification in Edwards's six-page preface to the whole.[24] There he defends the "old protestant doctrine" against the "new-fashioned divinity"—Arminianism—that raised such an "unusual ruffle" in the minds of his parishioners with talk of "speculative niceties, and subtle distinctions." Doctrines may be "clear and rational" and still need "diligence and attention of mind" to understand them; indeed, while the first principles of Christianity "contain something that is easy, yet they also contain great mysteries." Clear distinctions warranted by Scripture help open those mysteries. And a plain style keeps them that way. Ornament and elegance mean little to a congregation "deeply impressed" by their need for salvation; a "very plain and unpolished dress" suits them better, Edwards contends. Besides, he is unable to write "politely." And God seems to approve: "[H]e has been pleased to smile upon and bless a very plain unfashionable way of preaching."

The text for the sermon, "But to him that worketh not, but believeth on him that justifieth the ungodly, his faith is counted for righteousness" (Rom. 4:5), sets out the terms of the doctrine plainly in the contrast between what a man does and what he believes, between his works and his faith. Covenant or federal theology held that God made an agreement, a covenant, with Adam, offering him (and, as the head of mankind, his posterity) eternal happiness if he would labor to obey the divine injunction, God's freely given promise for the active, not simply the passive, obedience to His law: a covenant of works. Adam disobeyed God, his original sin, forfeited the covenant of works, and earned for himself (and us) eternal damnation: "In Adam's fall / We sinned all," recited the children of *The New-England Primer.* But God, by His sovereign will and in a free act of love for man, offered Abraham (and his seed) a new covenant, one fixed on faith, and gave His only begotten Son to satisfy the old covenant and to justify, that is, forgive, man's sins: a covenant of grace. Edwards's doctrine puts it succinctly: "We are justified only by faith in Christ, and not by any manner of virtue or goodness of our own."

The rest of the sermon—really two expanded public lectures of 130 pages—dwells on the meaning, truth, and demands of justification, often turning to verbal analysis beyond the customary explication of the text to make the point. Thus the word *justified*—"a forensic term" with implications for the law—not only connotes slightly different meanings as befits its "etymology and natural import," but it also agrees with "the force of the word as used in scripture"; the phrase "justification by faith" creates "great difficulty" for many believers, chiefly because of "the import and force of the particle *by*"; and the consequent notion, "by faith alone," more nearly means union or relation with Christ—"If any are disgusted at the word *union,* as obscure and unintelligible, the word *relation* equally serves my purpose"—rendered in the Bible by metaphors of body, tree, or marriage.

For the truth of the doctrine, Edwards turns not to semantics but to logic and, again, as he must, to Scripture. There is "a great deal of absurdity and self-contradiction" to the schemes of the Arminians, he begins. They hold not only that the covenant of works, which required perfect obedience, has been replaced by the covenant of grace, which requires imperfect obedience—how, they ask, can a just God require more of fallen man?—but also that Christ died to satisfy those very imperfections and make them acceptable to God. "Now," Edwards asks, "how can these things hang together?" If our imperfections break no law, they are not sins; if they are not sins, then Christ died for nothing. If they are sins, what law did they break? "They cannot be a breach of their new law, for that requires no other than imperfect obedience, or obedience with imperfections; and they cannot be a breach of the old law, for that they say is entirely abolished, and we never were under it; and we cannot break a law that we never were under." Scriptural proof of justification abounds, especially in the teaching of Paul: "There is no one doctrine that he insists so much upon, and is so particular in, and that he handles with so much distinctness, explaining and giving reasons, and answering objections." All of it makes clear that works share no part in justification, not ceremonial law or moral law, not obedience, or virtue, or righteousness. To share in justification "diminishes" God's grace, compromises Christ's sacrifice, and makes man "his own Saviour." Finally, justification demands acts of "positive" and "perfect" obedience, a first act of faith and perseverance in it, "an evangelical childlike, believing obedience."

Before closing with the uses of the doctrine and its "very great importance," Edwards, like Paul, answers objections, here those of "modern divines" and a few nettlesome texts, especially one from James 3:24, "Ye see then how that by works a man is justified, and not by faith only." Edwards resolves the obvious scriptural contradiction to his doctrine (and the "great unfairness" of those who cite it) in the ambiguity of the word *justify*. To justify, "in common speech," means either to approve or to testify to approval, "sometimes one, and sometimes the other. And that because they are both the same, only one is outwardly what the other is inwardly." James seems to use the word outwardly to mean *"manifestative justification,"* much as a tree manifests itself by its fruit. *Works,* in this context, means evidences or signs of justification, not the way to it. And so Edwards ends his argument much as he began it, defining words and attacking an "adverse scheme," carefully separating his people from their error, "which they may have been led into by education, or cunning sophistry of others," and which may be "contrary to the prevailing dispositions of their hearts, and contrary to their practice." Misunderstandings may account for that, and imprecise terms; if the doctrine of justification were "clearly explained," it would be embraced; certainly, "great allowances are to be made." Still, "it is manifest, from what has been said, that the teaching and propagating contrary doctrines and schemes"—he has Arminianism in mind—"is of a pernicious and fatal tendency."

Urgent pleas and "diverse excellencies." The next three discourses in the collection are shorter than "Justification by Faith Alone," less doctrinal and schismatic, and far more urgent. Edwards devotes two-thirds of the forty-page "Pressing into the Kingdom of God" (Luke 16:16) to the application or uses of the sermon, giving directions, naming the ways, exhorting his parishioners to open themselves to God's "gracious visitation" in "this town" this day, to *"let all go,"* to forget the past, to *"count the cost"* in the business of salvation, to invest prudently in "spiritual property." As their minister, "as one set over you," he beseeches them, "whether young or old, small or great," to declare themselves now, when the "state of the nation, and of this land, never looked so threatening," when God is now "gathering in his elect" before his awful judgment.[25] "Ruth's Resolution" (Ruth 1:16), to cleave to God and His people in calamitous times, ends like "Pressing into the Kingdom of God" with a plea to the young, but Edwards includes the very young here, as he does sometime later when he narrates the history of the Northampton revivals. "And you who are children, there have lately been some of your sort who have repented of their sins, loved the Lord Jesus Christ, and trusted in him, and are become God's children, as we have reason to hope. Let it stir you up to resolve to your utmost to seek and cry to God."[26] He returns to the Pauline epistle of "Justification by Faith Alone" in the third of these sermons, "The Justice of God in the Damnation of Sinners," with a text from the third chapter of Romans, a particular favorite of his. "I never found so much immediate saving fruit, in any measure, of any discourses I have offered to my congregation," he remarks elsewhere,[27] "as some from those words, Rom. 3:19, 'That every mouth may be

stopped'; endeavoring to shew from thence that it would be just with
God forever to reject and cast off mere natural men." Though both
sermons weigh God's justice, the tone differs dramatically as Edwards
abandons academic discourse for practical homiletics, head for heart.[28]
"Justification by Faith Alone" brushed truth with terror in the peroration—"wallowing, like filthy swine, in the mire of our sins"—and had
questioned the price of virtue. "But seeing we are such infinitely sinful
and abominable creatures in God's sight, and by our infinite guilt have
brought ourselves into such wretched and deplorable circumstances,
and all our righteousness are nothing, and ten thousand times worse
than nothing, (if God looks upon them as they be in themselves) is it
not immensely more worthy of the infinite majesty and glory of God,
to deliver and make happy such wretched vagabonds and captives,
without any money or price of theirs, or any manner or expectation of
excellency or virtue in them, in any wise to recommend them?" Now,
in his "joint consideration" of man's sinfulness and God's sovereignty,
Edwards pelts his listeners with imprecations in a hail of exclamation
points. "How sensual have you been! Are there not some here that have
debased themselves below the dignity of human nature, by wallowing
in sensual filthiness, as swine in the mire, or as filthy vermin feeding
with delight on rotten carrion? What intemperance have some of you
been guilty of! . . . And what abominable lasciviousness have some of
you been guilty of! How have you indulged yourself from day to day,
and from night to night, in all manner of unclean imaginations! Has
not your soul been filled with them, till it has become a hold of foul
spirits, and a cage of every unclean and hateful bird?" Man violated
"infinite obligations," an "infinitely heinous" crime, deserving "infinite punishment"; is himself "a mere earthworm," "a filthy worm," "a
poor little worm," "a worm, a mere nothing, and less than nothing."
But the "infinitely lovely" divine sovereign offers nothing man all in
Christ. "Of such dignity and excellency is Christ in the eyes of God,
that, seeing he has suffered so much for poor sinners, God is willing
to be at peace with them, however vile and unworthy they have been,
and on how many accounts soever the punishment would be just."

The last of the discourses on salvation echoes those lines from "The
Justice of God in the Damnation of Sinners," though not its threat,
and closes the book on a more hopeful verse, John's vision of the lion
and the lamb in Rev. 5:5–6. "The Excellency of Jesus Christ"[29] was
preached much earlier—August 1728—and added here on Edwards's
"own notion" to complement the "awakening" sermons before it and

to answer a petition of "another town" to publish it. Edwards takes the double image of the lion and the lamb to be the central paradox of Jesus as man-god. Christ is an "'admirable conjunction of diverse excellencies,'" as the doctrine puts it, a "wonderful conjunction" of justice and mercy, of "infinite majesty and transcendent meekness," of reverence for God and equality with Him, of "absolute sovereignty and perfect resignation." These excellencies meet in Christ's incarnation, life, and passion, both in His exaltation in heaven and His acts at the Last Judgment. They are there now, Edwards offers, for those who seek Him. "Be you never so wicked a creature, here is worthiness enough. Be you never so poor, and mean, and ignorant a creature, there is no danger of being despised; for though he be so much greater than you, he is immensely more humble than you." And there, in Christ's duality, in the divine and the human, lies man's prospect for the triadic union of John's promise (Rev. 17:21–23). "Christ has brought it to pass that those that the Father has given him should be brought into the household of God; that he and his Father, and his people, should be, as it were, one society, one family; that the church should be as it were admitted into the society of the blessed Trinity."

Discourses on Various Important Subjects was published in 1738, ten years after Edwards first delivered "The Excellency of Jesus Christ" and three years or so after he first delivered the other four sermons, sometime between the late fall of 1734 and the late spring of 1735. The collection left to later editors the publishing of two other sermons Edwards preached in the same period to much the same purpose. In May, he took as texts Luke 17:32, "Remember Lot's wife," and 1 Thess. 2:16, "To fill up their sins alway; for the wrath is come upon them to the uttermost." Both score unrepentant sinners, in the Old Testament and in Northampton, especially in a season of the spirit. The first of them, "The Folly of looking back in fleeing out of Sodom," warns those "in this land of light" to escape sin as they would Sodom, the city "typified" by it, and to join their neighbors in repentance now. "The wonders that we have seen among us of late, have been of a more glorious nature than those that the children of Israel saw in Egypt and in the wilderness."[30] The second, "When the Wicked shall have filled the Measure of their Sin, Wrath will come upon them to the uttermost," repeats the parallel. "God appears among us in the most extraordinary manner, perhaps, that ever he did in New-England. The children of Israel saw many mighty works of God, when he brought them out of Egypt; but we, at this day, see works more mighty, and

of a more glorious nature." At times, the words call up an earlier sermon—"you were warned to flee from wrath, and were urged to press
into the Kingdom of God"; at times, they call up a lovely image from
Isa. (60:8)—"You have seen persons daily flocking to Christ, as doves
to their windows"; at times, an image of fear and terror—"Sometimes,
when God only enlightens conscience, to have some sense of his wrath,
it causes the stout-hearted to cry out; . . . how must it be when God
opens the flood-gates, and lets the mighty deluge of his wrath come
pouring down upon men's guilty heads, and brings in all his waves
and billows upon their souls! How little of God's wrath will sink
them!"[31]

Harvests of Change

Two letters, one narrative. On 30 May, Edwards wrote in reply
to the Rev. Dr. Benjamin Colman, pastor of the Brattle Street Church
in Boston, about the "present extraordinary circumstances" of the
Northampton revivals. Before he sent it off, he added this on 3 June:
"Since I wrote the foregoing Letter, there has Happen'd a thing of a
very awful nature in the Town; My Uncle Hawley, the Last Sabbath
day morning, Laid violent Hands on himself, & Put an End to his Life,
by Cutting his own throat." Later that week, Edwards "appointed a
day of Fasting in the Town"; later that month, he preached on Ps.
46:10, "Be still, and know that I am God."[32]
    A *Faithful Narrative Of The Surprising Work of God In The Conversion
Of Many Hundred Souls in Northampton, and the Neighboring Towns and
Villages of the County of Hampshire, in the Province of the Massachusetts-Bay
in New-England* grew to 132 pages by the time it was published in
London in 1737.[33] Colman had sent extracts of Edwards's eight-page
letter to a London correspondent, the Rev. Dr. John Guyse, who shared
them with his congregation and with Isaac Watts, the hymnist and a
fellow Dissenting minister. Their pleasure with the extracts, and
Guyse's desire to publish them, persuaded Colman to ask Edwards—
indirectly, through his aging uncle, the Rev. William Williams of
Hatfield—for a fuller account. Edwards told Northampton about it—
"I read that part of your letter to the congregation"—and by 6 November 1737 had complied with Colman's request in a long, detailed letter. Colman reduced it to nineteen pages, appended the abridgment to
Williams's *The Duty and Interest of a People* (and another of his evangelical sermons), and had it on the Boston streets and off to London by

mid-December. In late February, and again in early April, Watts implored Colman to publish the whole of it—"we have not heard anything like it since the Reformation, nor perhaps since the days of the apostles"—and pledged five pounds to see it in print. But the Boston publication of the whole narrative proved impolitic—perhaps the Williamses, bitter rivals of Edwards, prevailed upon the local printers—and so Colman shipped the entire manuscript to Watts sometime before the first of May. By mid-October the text was at the printers, edited, with a fourteen-page preface by Guyse and Watts and with a title of their own making. The book was published by John Oswald "at the Rose and Crown" and, a year later, in Boston by Samuel Kneeland and Timothy Green "over against the Prison in Queen-street." Within a year it was translated into German; within three, into Dutch. Over the next hundred years it was issued more than two dozen times in an effort, as Watts had earlier hoped, "to spread this narrative in the world."[34]

Edwards's letter to the world reads more like history and theology and psychology than glad tidings, more like a treatise on Calvin and Locke than correspondence. As historian, Edwards documents times and places, connects past to present, factors change; as pastor, he confirms the "late wonderful work of God" in the morphology of conversion, counting the steps of the awakened; and as soul physician, he reports cases of conscience, especially in the young, and charts the course of symptoms in clinical detail. Here, in his retelling of the conversion experiences of so many, are his teachings of the last half-dozen years made real: the divine sovereignty of *God Glorified*; the special grace (and cautions) of "Justification by Faith Alone"; the pilgrimage of "The True Christian's Life"; the terrors and "The Torments of the Wicked in Hell"; and the sweetness and "The Excellency of Jesus Christ." Here is the evangelical pattern and the ministerial role that will be imitated—and parodied—in the next awakening in America and the next and the next and the next. And here, as in his letter on spiders, he asks to be judged tenderly. "I am sensible the practice [of certifying conversion] would have been safer in the hands of a riper judgment and greater experience."

Six months, a marked falling off of the spirit, the prospect of an audience abroad—all these separate the two letters and may account for the change.[35] After a few words of acknowledgement in the first letter—expanded tenfold in the second—Edwards launches into the subject close at hand, a lively eyewitness. "I have observed that the

Town for this several years have gradually been Reforming; There has appeared Less & Less of a party spirit, & a contentious disposition, which before had Prevail'd for many years between two Parties in the Town. The young People also have been Reforming more and more; They by degrees Left off their frolicking, and have been observably more decent in their attendance on Publick worship." The second letter begins with a history of Northampton and Hampshire county, a school-book of geography—"Our being so far within the land, at a distance from seaports"—and sociology, of pulpit succession and the seasons of conversion—"harvests, as [Solomon Stoddard] called them." Only after that formal introduction does Edwards write of the young and the "sensible amendment" of their ways. "At the latter end of the year 1733, there appeared a very unusual flexibleness and yielding to advice, in our young people." Then the narrative settles into many of the details of the earlier letter: the "very sudden and awful death of a young man in the bloom of his youth" in April 1734; the death of a young married woman shortly after; the growing religious convictions of the young; and their meetings "in various parts of town" after Sunday lecture by the fall (and at Edwards's suggestion).

"About this time, began the great noise that was in this part of the country about Arminianism, which seemed to appear with a very threatening aspect" and which Edwards tried to silence with lectures on justification by faith. "And then it was, in the latter part of December, that the Spirit of God began extraordinarily," and then it was that "very suddenly" six converted, among them "one of the greatest company-keepers in the whole town." The good news struck like "a flash of lightning, upon the hearts of young people all over the town" and then upon others, so that by the summer of 1735 "scarcely a single person in town, either old or young was left unconcerned," children and parents, husbands and wives, all now singing with "unusual elevation of heart and voice." Edwards records the spread of the revival to neighboring towns—an epic catalogue of thirty-two communities and twenty-nine ministers, his father and East Windsor among them—and throughout his parish, three hundred converts in half a year, the elderly and the very young, two above seventy, one about four years old, Phebe Bartlet.[36]

The morphology of conversion. Edwards promises to return with a "particular account" of her incredible story, but for now, and for fully half the text, he will describe the natural history of conversion as he observed it, because, critics aside, he doesn't take "every religious

pang and enthusiastic conceit for saving conversion." A pattern of conversion had been part of Puritan New England almost from the beginning, if not with the Separatists of Plimouth Plantation then certainly
by 1640 with the non-Separatists of Massachusetts Bay, and though
the exact number of steps varied from minister to minister the overall
order and direction did not. First came attendance upon the ministry
of God's word and next an understanding of God's law, or the nature
of good and evil. Later, this general understanding narrowed to a particular awareness of personal sinfulness, what the Puritans called a conviction of sin or humiliation, a condition marked by fear and faith and
polarities of doubt. Profound despair set in, and hard upon it—and in
endless counterpoint—a cry for forgiveness. Assurance came then, that
God would be merciful, and so came unmerited saving grace. None of
this was certain, of course—"to be sure one must be unsure"—but
much of it was visible—the humility, the calling, the doubts, the walk
with God. And Edwards in Northampton had seen it at first hand,
many times over.[37]

He saw the conviction of sin, the "awful apprehensions persons have
had of their misery," which came upon some suddenly, "as if their
hearts were pierced through with a dart," and upon others gradually,
in meditation and in thought. The effect was immediate and sustained:
"it was no longer the tavern, but the minister's house, that was
thronged." Some had been encouraged from their first awakening, and
had "ten times less trouble of mind"; some had been "scarcely free from
terror" through countless sleepless nights. Melancholy afflicted some,
"in which Satan probably has a great hand," while others neared "the
borders of despair." For most, as their conviction deepened and as they
fell headlong upon the "unpardonable sin," willfully turning away
from spiritual truth, there arose in them an absolute dependence on
God's sovereign power, on Christ's mediation, and on "remarkably
blessed" sermons like "The Justice of God in the Damnation of Sinners." "Thus they wander about from mountain to hill, seeking rest
and finding none: when they are beat out of one refuge they fly to
another, till they are as it were debilitated, broken, and subdued with
legal humblings; in which God gives them conviction of their own
utter helplessness and insufficiency, and discovers the true remedy."
But their time of trial differed—a few days, months, years—for, as
Edwards explains, God does not limit Himself "to any certain method
in his proceedings."[38]

Nor does He confine Himself "to certain steps, and a particular

method" in the discovery of grace. Sometimes it was through a particular scriptural text or texts, or none; sometimes in a changed apprehension of things, by sight or gradually in the heart; sometimes in
Christ's dying love, in His obedience, His loveliness, His divinity. At
times, a sense of unworthiness left some "like trees in winter, or like
seed in the spring suppressed under a hard clod of earth." When the
light of conversion came, it came with a sudden flash of glory to some,
but to others, "like the dawning of day, when at first but a little light
appears," hiding behind a cloud, "till at length, perhaps, it breaks
forth more clearly." Some could recall the precise moment it came,
others not even the date. But all agreed that it brought with it a new
sense of things, as when, for the first time, their eyes were opened to
the sun "in the midst of a clear hemisphere, and the strong blaze of his
light overcomes all objectives against his being." Then they saw and
felt and "tasted" the things of religion, the truth of the Gospel, and
the need for preaching, "and they wonder that they did not see 'em
before." Like Edwards in "Personal Narrative," written probably
within two years of this account, they enjoy a light that "causes all
things about 'em to appear as it were beautiful, sweet and pleasant to
them: all things abroad, the sun, moon and stars, the clouds and sky,
the heavens and earth, appear as it were with a cast of divine glory and
sweetness upon them." They long for Christ, and they talk, "when
able to speak," of the glory of God, "annihilating themselves" before
Him. Others imagine hell and have "lively ideas of a dreadful furnace";
still others imagine Christ and have a "lively idea of Christ hanging
upon the cross, and his blood running from his wounds." There is a
"vast difference" in the degree and manner of conversions, an "endless
variety" of personal experiences, and Edwards cites a few of them in
the course of his narrative: "Here was a remarkable instance of an aged
woman, that had spent most of her days under Mr. Stoddard's powerful
ministry"; "There are some persons that I have been acquainted with,
but more especially two, that belong to other towns"; "it was particularly remarkable in one, who having been taken captive in his childhood was trained up in Canada in the popish religion." In the main,
however, he deals in *some* and *sometimes,* the language of generic experience, and only at the very end of the narrative in names, Abigail
Hutchinson and Phebe Bartlet.[39]

    Two cases of conscience.   Although he admits to "a very broken
and imperfect account" of the conversion of Abigail Hutchinson, a
young woman "infirm of body," Edwards logs her progress in some

detail from the onset of her awakening "on Monday" in late December 1734 to her death "about noon, on Friday, June 27, 1735." On learning of the conversion of "one of the greatest company-keepers in the whole town," she resolved to read the Bible through in search of the principles of religion and the ways of salvation, but by Thursday she abandoned the project, turning instead to the New Testament for "relief there for her distressed soul." By Saturday "her eyes were so dim that she could not know the letters"; by Sunday she was too weak to go to church. Monday she felt "a constant sweetness in her soul," but later that week, relating (and reliving) it, she collapsed and was put to bed. She gave Edwards a day-to-day account of her sense of Christ's glory, and " a kind of beatific vision of God," which, as she explained to her sister, she often saw in nature, in "'the wind blowing the trees.'" She had "great longings to die," to be with Christ, but, thinking more on it, decided to submit to God's will, whether to live or die. "After this her illness increased upon her." Her throat swelled; she could not eat for the "strugglings and stranglings"; she grew worse; the flesh "dried upon her bones." She died "in an admirable sweet composure." She said, "'God has shewed me that he can make it easy in great pain.'" Edwards said, "She was looked upon amongst us, as a very eminent instance of Christian experience."

Phebe Bartlet's awakening began about two months before Abigail Hutchinson's death, in late April or early May, a month or so after she turned four and shortly after her brother's conversion at eleven. A secondhand though truthful account, Edwards tells us, it is derived "from the mouths of her parents." Phebe would retire to her closet "five or six times a day" for secret prayer, but on the last Thursday in July her mother overheard these words "(spoken in her childish manner, but seemed to be spoken with extraordinary earnestness, and out of distress of soul): 'Pray, blessed Lord, give me salvation! I pray, beg, pardon all my sins!'" Later, out of the closet, she wept, "'Yes, I am afraid I shall go to hell!'"; later still, she smiled, "'Mother, the kingdom of heaven is come to me!'" Friday, she cried over her three older sisters—"Poor Nabby!" "Poor Eunice!" "Poor Amy!"—fearing they would go to hell; Saturday, she had "four turns of crying"; Sunday, she longed "to hear Mr. Edwards preach." In August, after a plum raid in a neighbor's lot with the bigger children, she was "mildly reproved" by her mother but stayed disconsolate, having sinned, and "retained her aversion for that fruit for a considerable time." In September, husking Indian corn with her sisters, she entreated them to pray, to prepare to die, to be "always ready"; in November, she spoke to them of Rev. 3:20, an invitation to be saved. In the middle of winter, "very late in the night," she wept aloud for Christ's love of her and lay awake restless. At the time of his writing, Edwards reports, she continues in secret prayer, in nightly catechism, and in "great love to her minister."

An end to the affair. Had they the choice, Guyse and Watts remarked in their preface to the London edition, they would have illustrated the wonderful work of God with two cases "of more significancy in the eye of the world" than those of Abigail Hutchinson and Phebe Bartlet, especially the last. "Children's language," they pointed out, "always loses its striking beauties at secondhand." Still, whatever the "supposed imperfection" of the narrative, they heartily endorsed both the surprising work that gave rise to it and the "worthy writer" who recorded it. Their American counterparts voiced no qualms about cases or language. In the preface to the Boston edition, the Reverends Joseph Sewall, Thomas Prince, John Webb, and William Cooper earnestly hoped that publication of the narrative would promote conversion "throughout the land" and its "worthy author" continue "a rich blessing to his people!" And six Hampshire County ministers, "eye and ear witnesses," as they called themselves, attested that Edwards's account of their towns was "true"—Hatfield, Suffield, Longmeadow, Enfield, Westfield, West Springfield. All the ministers had read the final section of his narrative, had known the deepening melancholy in their towns, and had seen the revival slip from his hands to his dead uncle's.

By late spring, Edwards wrote, "a poor weak man" tried to cut his throat, and a "useful honorable person" succeeded in cutting his. The "disease of melancholy" struck "multitudes" in Northampton and neighboring towns, quickened them to despair, cried to them, "'Cut your own throat, now is a good opportunity: *now, NOW!*'" Some were caught up in "strange enthusiastic delusions," one man believing he had the gifts of the Holy Ghost, something, Edwards was quick to add, reserved for ministers. Conversions slowed then, and "the Spirit of God not long after this, appeared very sensibly withdrawing from all parts of the county." Events conspired to turn the people away: the governor's visit to Deerfield to treat with the Indians; the building of a new meetinghouse in Northampton and the fussing about pews; and the notorious Breck affair in Springfield, which "doubtless above all things" brought the revival to an end. But hundreds who were converted during it remained so, and not a young person in town returned to "looseness and extravagancy." A few may have been "stumbled" by false professions, but most narratives were, by every human measure, faithful. "[W]e are," Edwards claims, "evidently a people blessed of the Lord! And here, in this corner of the world, God dwells and manifests his glory." Of Colman he asks only prayers for the town and for himself, "Your obedient son and servant."[40]

Divine Wrath and Christian Love

The enmity of natural man. A chastened stillness fell upon his pulpit. In June he preaches a bleak sermon on God's sovereignty, "The sole consideration, that God is God, sufficient to still all objections to his Sovereignty" (Ps. 46:10), without a word about Northampton or the suicide it knew; in January, at a time of "epidemical sickness" nearby, he again turns to Psalms (45:2) in "The Most High a Prayer-hearing God," and again no word about Northampton and the sin-sickness he had diagnosed. By April the light of the late awakening had fled, even if the need for it had not. The "surest" way to know God, Edwards asserts in "God the best Portion of the Christian" (Ps. 73:25), is by a "feeling of some particular, strong, and lively exercise" of the spirit, with or without his help. "At such times the people of God do not need any help of ministers to satisfy them whether they have the true love of God; they plainly see and feel it."[41]

The following month and in four sermons in August, he turns from the sovereignty of God to the obverse doctrine, the enmity of natural man. In "Unbelievers contemn the Glory and Excellency of Christ" (Acts 4:11), he scores the "heinousness of the sin of *unbelief*" and exults in a just God denying Christ to such sinners. "How justly might you be refused any part in that precious stone, whose preciousness you make no account of, and esteem no more than that of the stones of the street!" He defines man's apostasy in "Men naturally God's Enemies" (Rom. 5:10) as the rejection of God for other gods, for the idols of self and things. "Man has naturally a principle of Atheism in him; an indisposition to realize God's being, and a disposition to doubt it. The being of God does not ordinarily seem real to natural men." Their enmity darkens their judgments, wills, affections, and practices, their faculties and their principles. But God's restraining grace, another measure of divine sovereignty, keeps them from the unpardonable sin and proffers them love through the dying Christ. Thus God loves His enemies; so men, taught in His ways, should love theirs. "And we ought to love them even while enemies; for so we hope God hath done to us. We should be the children of our Father, who is kind to the unthankful and evil." In September, metaphors of darkness and light, of the sea-drowned and the saved, of lost travellers and found make their way through a sermon preached on conviction, "Hope and Comfort Follow Genuine Humiliation and Repentance" (Hosea 2:15), just as a single metaphor, God's house, builds "The Many Mansions" (John 14:2), a sermon on the Sunday following the seating of the new church in Northampton, 25 December 1737. Both sermons contrast sharply with the scrubbed logic of the August series on enmity.[42]

In the spring of 1738, Edwards returned to the subject he all but abandoned three years earlier, the Northampton revivals. He breaks through the calm of "Jesus Christ the Same Yesterday, To-day, and For Ever" (Heb. 13:8) with peals of reproof.

And though Christ be unchangeable, yet you are not. You have changed for the worse, since the time when you were awakened. . . . Christ's wrath hung over your head then, and so it does now, but with this difference, that now much more of that wrath hangs over you than did then. You hung over the pit of hell then, and so you do now; but with this difference, that you have ever since been kindling and enraging the flames of that fiery gulf over which you hang, so that they are vastly fiercer than they were then; and the moth of time has been nibbling at that slender thread ever since, and has much nearer gnawed it off than it had been.

Townspeople were "full of praises" for Christ then, but now, dumb to anthems, they have wandered off to riches, amusements, "fine clothes and gay apparel," have changed so, as Christ assuredly has not. "Are we so foolish as to think that he, that is the same yesterday, to-day, and for ever, is so much altered from what he was three years ago?"[43]

Rebukes like that ring down "Joseph's great Temptation, and gracious Deliverance" (Gen. 39:12), but here Edwards decries the particular temptations of the young, "different sexes lying in bed together!" and "getting together in the night, in those companies for mirth and jollity, that they call frolics; so spending time together till late in the night, in their jollity." He recalls that time "two or three years ago" when they sought out each other for prayer. Puzzled now, he asks, "And what is the matter? Why did you not set up the practice then, when your heart was taken up about reading, meditation, and secret prayer to God? If this do not all stand in the way of them, and is no hindrance to them, why was you not engaged in both together? What account can you give of it? Why did you leave off this practice and custom, or abstain from it? To what purpose is this changing?" He hopes—"I desire" is the regular verb of his frustration—that the heads of families would govern more closely and, without abridging "proper liberties," curtail the mischief.[44]

By summer, failing answers, he is aloft with a vision. "Jesus Christ Gloriously exalted above all Evil, in the Work of Redemption" (1 Cor. 15:25–26), an August lecture, begins with a two-page history of redemption, from Satan's fall to the rise of the Antichrist, and then sweeps to Christ's triumph over evil as "a mighty Deluge" and "a boundless Ocean," "an immense Fountain of Light, that with the fulness and abundance of His Brightness, swallows up Men's greatest Sins, as little Motes are swallowed up and hidden in the Disk of the Sun." Later, in the application, Christ soars over "God's Waves and Billows" with the redeemed, "as on Eagles Wings, high out of Reach of all Evils, so that they cannot come near them, so as to do them any real Harm. And in a little time, they shall be carried so out of their Reach, that they shall not be able ever to molest them any more for ever."[45] Within a year the doctrine of Christ's redemptive power caught his imagination again, not in one sermon but in many, not on the wings of metaphor but in a chronicle of world history.

The love of Christ.   Before embarking on that history, indeed before the close of 1738, Edwards preached sixteen sermons on charity, "apparently designed by himself for publication; for they were written out in full." Even so, they remained in manuscript another hundred years until his great-grandson, the Rev. Dr. Tryon Edwards, published them in 1852 as *Charity and Its Fruits*.[46] The sermons—lectures, really—explicate the thirteenth chapter of first Corinthians, the apostle Paul's definitions of Christian love that begins in discord—"Though I speak with the tongue of men and angels and have not charity, I am become a sounding brass or a tinkling cymbal"—and ends in simple affirmation—"And now abideth faith, hope, charity, these three; but the greatest of these is charity." Although Edwards comments upon the whole of the chapter (and upon other chapters in the epistle besides), the text for the series is the first ten verses only, such that in Lectures I–III he comments upon verses 1–3, the sum of charity; in IV–VI upon verse 4, the fruits of charity; in VIII–X upon verse 5, the spirit of charity; in XI–XIV upon verses 6–7, the practice of charity; and in XV–XVI upon verses 8–10, the end of charity. Each lecture begins with a summary and a prospect, and then, in standard triadic form, opens a text, explains the doctrine, and urges its application.

In the fourth lecture, for instance, Edwards recalls the text and sub-ject of the first three lectures and suggests the next two. He divides the text, the first sentence of the fourth verse, explicating the first part for this lecture, "Charity suffereth long," and reserving to the fifth lecture the second part, "and is kind." Numbering the injuries Chris-tians suffer, from "unreasonable prices" to authority "magisterially and tyrannically" imposed, he argues the duty of forbearance, the need to suffer without revenge or anger, through inward calm and "for the sake of peace." Charity, he concludes, disposes Christians to suffer, much as a loving parent suffers "many things in his own child that he would greatly reprobate in the child of another." Christ, of course, is the example: meekness and repose and suffering, out of love for God and man. For those who unwillingly submit to intolerable, repeated, and unpunished injuries, Edwards interposes God—"Do you think that the injuries from your fellow-man are more than you have offered to God?"—and Rom. 12:19 on divine vengeance. The lecture ends in hope and ambivalence: "Cherish, then, the spirit of longsuffering, meekness, and forbearance, and you shall possess your soul in patience and happiness, and none shall be permitted to harm you more than God in wisdom and kindness may permit."

The other lectures are fashioned in much the same way, plainly in-structive, logical, heavy with Scripture. Doctrinal concerns of the 1730s filter through, as in this on imputation and justification in the fourteenth lecture:

When Adam fell, he was condemned, and all his posterity was condemned with him, and fell with him. But if he had stood, he would have been justi-fied, and so would have partaken of the tree of life, and been confirmed in a state of life, and all his posterity would have been confirmed. And, by parity of reason, now that Christ, the second Adam, has stood and persevered, and is justified, and confirmed in life, all who are in Christ and represented by him, are also accepted, and justified, and confirmed in him. The fact that he, as the covenant-head of his people, has fulfilled the terms of the covenant, makes it sure that they shall persevere.[47]

In the fifth lecture, Edwards connects charity to free will: "The proper and conclusive evidence of our wishing or willing to do good to another is, to do it"; in the second lecture, to the divine and supernatural light: "All the fruits of the Spirit, which we are to lay weight upon as evidential of grace, are summed up in charity." And in the first lecture, months before he would undertake his elaborate history, he connects charity to redemption: "The work of redemption which the gospel makes known, above all things affords motives to love; for that work was the most glorious and wonderful exhibition of love that ever was seen or heard of." It was also, Edwards would soon make plain, the divine connection in time, God's grand design of history.

Redemption through Time

Divinity as history.   From March to August 1739, Edwards devoted his pulpit to a series of sermons on the history of the work of redemption. He continued to preach on other doctrinal matters, of course—on the promise of damnation in "The Eternity of Hell Torments" (Matt. 25:46) in April and on the necessity of intolerance in "The Nature and End of Excommunication" (1 Cor. 5:11) in July, for example[48]—but for a good part of half a year he thought and wrote and spoke about redemption as history. Thirty-five years later, his son gathered these manuscript sermons and with the editorial help of the Rev. Dr. John Erskine, his father's principal correspondent in Scotland, had them published there, not, he remarks in the preface, without misgiving. His father had neither prepared the sermons for the press—though it is clear from his notebooks that he returned to them often—nor had he the "elegance of composition, which is now esteemed so essential to all publications." Still, he shows "plain good sense" in these pages, "real unfeigned piety" and "sentiments uncommon"; perhaps that, his son suggests, might make up for a prose "destitute of the ornaments of fine language." Thus *A History of the Work of Redemption* was published in Edinburgh and London in 1774, altered in its divisions to form a "continued treatise," notes Erskine, an octavo volume of nearly four hundred pages.[49] Over the course of the next hundred years and twenty-five printings, it was published in Boston, New York, Dublin, Utrecht, Toulouse, Bala, and Beirut; in Dutch, French, Welsh, and Arabic.

Edwards thought this project "a great work," as he wrote the Princeton trustees from Stockbridge in 1757, "a Body of Divinity in an entire new method, being thrown into the form of an history." He planned to trace the work of redemption by Christ, "the grand design, of all God's designs, and the summum and ultimum of all the divine operations and decrees," through historical time, ordering acts and events and the "revolutions in the world of mankind" from the beginning to the final judgment, linking worlds together, heaven and earth and hell, refracting history through the prism of the Word. To Edwards this new method seemed "the most beautiful and entertaining, wherein every divine doctrine, will appear to the greatest advantage in the brightest light, in the most striking manner showing the admirable contexture and harmony of the whole."[50] To Erskine, looking back, it seemed a more modest affair, not the abstruse or unduly metaphysical Edwards he and other readers knew, but a book meant to instruct and improve "ordinary Christians." The *History* shares both Edwards's claim and Erskine's in a familiar mix of the new with the old.

Definitions and parallels. The text for the whole of it is Isa. 51:8, "For the moth shall eat them up like a garment, and the worm shall eat them like wool: but my righteousness shall be for ever, and my salvation from generation to generation." After three pages of explication, Edwards arrives at the doctrine, "The work of redemption is a work that God carries on from the fall of man to the end of the world." But before going on to the history proper, he pauses to define two terms in the doctrine and, by the way, reveals his philosophy of history. He takes the word *redemption* (or *salvation,* "the same thing") not in its "limited sense" as Christ's purchase of salvation on earth but "more largely" as all the works tending to it and from it. Limited to a time from Christ's incarnation to the day of His resurrection, the work of redemption would have ended then, he argues, "*virtually* done and finished." But it was not "*actually*" done and finished then, because there had been work "properly preparatory" to it and work successfully accomplished after it. Redemption, for Edwards, has to do with all time, with Christ on earth "or before, or since" and with the "confederated" work of the trinity from the beginning. It is "but one work, one design," much like the "several wheels" of one machine that "answer one end, and produce one effect." The second term, *carried on* (or *carrying on*), means that the work of redemption is going on still but will end—"all this while accomplishing"—like the "successive motions of one machine, to bring about in the conclusion one great event." The steps to salvation remain the same throughout history— conviction, justification, sanctification, glorification—and so redemption is carried on "by repeating and continually working the same work over again, though in different persons, from age to age." As in a Newtonian machine, an orrery or a time-piece, figures of redemption turn and turn to uniform laws in tireless succession from creation to apocalypse, the whole impelled onward, ascending. Each saving work, each moment of time is not only part of the whole but the pattern of it as well. By some divine calculus of redemption, each discrete event recreates in small God's grand design.

Edwards elaborates upon the parallel between individual and historical redemption and the uneven, though inevitable, progress of both, interrupting his life of Enoch early in the *History* to do so. "[T]he elect church in general, from the first erecting of the church to the end of the world, is very much after the same manner as the carrying on of the same work and the same light in a particular soul, from the time of its conversion, till it is perfected and crowned in glory. The work in a particular soul has its ups and downs; sometimes the light shines brighter, and sometimes it is a dark time." So it is with the "great affair" of history, a time of corruption, a time of grace, but ever the kingdom of Christ "building up" to perfect glory at the end of the world.[51]

Images of a grand design. The most common of images in any account of redemption, the gospel light often involves Edwards in metaphors of the sun, God's Son, and recalls, as it must, his delight in the *Opticks* of an earlier time: the slant of light of the just-risen sun, the burning light of the sun at the meridian, the reflected light of "other luminaries" at night, the fading light of the moon as it nears "conjunction" with the sun. These recur throughout the *History* to track the soul's changeable weather, a sort of farmer's almanac of redemption; but it is in the tropes of architecture, perhaps suggested by the new meetinghouse in town, that Edwards finds a language proper to its grand design.

Like an house or temple that is building; first, the workmen are sent forth, then the materials are gathered, then the ground fitted, then the foundation is laid, then the superstructure is erected, one part after another, till at length the top stone is laid, and all is finished. Now the work of redemption in that large sense that has been explained, may be compared to such a building, that is carrying on from the fall of man to the end of the world. God went about it immediately after the fall of man. Some things were done towards it immediately, as may be shown hereafter; and so God has proceeded, as it were, getting materials and building, ever since; and so will proceed to the end of the world; and then the time will come when the top stone shall be brought

forth, and all will appear complete and consummate. The glorious structure
will then stand forth in its proper perfection.

Another structure, the tower of Babel, also "belongs" to the grand
design but only to typify opposition: its foundation was laid "in the
pride and vanity of men, and the haughtiness of their minds, so it was
built on a foundation exceedingly contrary to the nature of the kingdom of Christ, and his redeemed city, which has its foundation laid in
humility."[52] On just such a biblical foundation of types, of temple and
tower, did Edwards erect his *History*.

Often the figures in it are highly wrought, the anti-type an intricate
play upon the type, as in this on the great flood of Genesis, later the
Red Sea of Exodus:

That water that washed away the filth of the world, that cleared the world of
wicked men, was a type of the blood of Christ, that takes away the sin of the
world. That water that delivered Noah and his sons from their enemies, is a
type of the blood that delivers God's church from their sins, their worst enemies. That water that was so plentiful and abundant, that it filled the world,
and reached above the tops of the highest mountains, was a type of that blood,
the sufficiency of which is so abundant, that it is sufficient for the whole
world; sufficient to bury the highest mountains of sin. The ark that was the
refuge and hiding-place of the church in this time of storm and flood, was a
type of Christ, the true hiding-place of the church, from the storms and floods
of God's wrath.

Edwards's reading here, however ingenious it seems, simply follows
the practice of reading the Bible symbolically in a manner first set
down by the early Church Fathers and continued in Reformist Europe
and Puritan America, in John Calvin's *Institutes of the Christian Religion*
(1536) and in Samuel Mather's *Figures or Types of the Old Testament*
(1683).[53] But Edwards had a habit of slipping the bonds of conven-
tional study, if not doctrine, and in the *History* he extended the reach
of traditional typology and its need for harmony in and between the
Old Testament and the New to include events outside both. Biblical
exegetes had done that before—Cotton Mather in *Magnalia Christi
Americana* (1702), for one, and "a certain very late expositor (Mr.
[Moses] Lowman)," for another—but Edwards tried to apply "a
method entirely new" to the whole of recorded past, not just parts of
it, wilderness New England or papal Rome. He very nearly succeeded.

A decade earlier, he found "images or shadows of divine things" in the world about him and wrote, sometime later, that the "book of Scripture is the interpreter of the book of nature.[54] Now he demonstrates that the book of Scripture is the interpreter of the book of history. In his analysis, hordes of invading Goths and Vandals in the fifth century represent Satan's attempt "to restore Paganism" to Rome, and their division of the western half of the empire into ten tribal kingdoms represents "the ten horns of the beast," or the Antichrist, and "the ten toes of Nebuchadnezzar's image, foretold in the 8th chapter of Revelation, in what came to pass under the sounding of the first four trumpets." Even in biblical times, between the Babylonian captivity and the coming of Christ, when there was no sacred or inspired history for more than four hundred years, "God in his providence took care, that there should be authentic and full accounts of the events of this period preserved in profane history" in order to reveal as fulfilled all the prophecies of Daniel and some in Isaiah, Jeremiah, and Ezekial. Under so thorough a reading as this, the mariner's compass becomes in Edwards's hands an instrument to thwart Satan by directing the gospel to heathens "how far soever off, and however separated by wide oceans."[55]

   Biblical history and secular. Edwards divides his *History* into three "very unequal" periods of redemption. The first, from the fall of man to the incarnation of Christ, is a time of preparation, of "forerunners and earnests" of redemption; the second, and shortest, from Christ's incarnation to His resurrection, is a time of purchase, "the most remarkable article of time that ever was or ever will be"; and the third, from Christ's resurrection to the end of the world, is a time of the effect and eventual success of redemption, "in the Old Testament called *the latter days.*" Each period is divided into parts or sections: six in the first (from the fall to the flood, to Abraham, Moses, David, the Babylonian captivity, and the coming of Christ); two in the second (the incarnation and the purchase); and seven in the third (to the destruction of Jerusalem, the reign of Constantine, the rise of the Antichrist, the Reformation, the present time, the fall of the Antichrist, and the end of time). To each period Edwards adds improvements or applications, and to the whole a "general" improvement, as in this encompassing figure near the end, a metaphor of streams and vantage points, God's and man's.

God's providence may not unfitly be compared to a large and long river, having innumerable branches, beginning in different regions, and at a great distance one from another, and all conspiring to one common issue. . . . The different streams of this river are apt to appear like mere jumble and confusion to us, because of the limitedness of our sight. . . . [A]t a distance there seem to be innumerable obstacles and impediments in the way to hinder their ever uniting and coming to the ocean, as rocks and mountains and the like; but yet if we trace them, they all unite at last, and all come to the same issue, disgorging themselves in one into the same great ocean. Not one of all the streams fail of coming hither at last.[56]

Such was the course of redemption Edwards descried from his pulpit then and, he expected, such it would remain until the millennium.

Like other Americans, Edwards's millennial hope followed the westering sun, out of Jerusalem to Rome, out of Geneva to New England, and with it the destruction of the Antichrist and the days of glory.[57] "It is now a very dark time," but "whether the times shall be any darker still, or how much darker, before the beginning of this glorious work of God, we cannot tell." That great work will come "very swiftly, yet gradually," as it has before, as it has recently in the "remarkable pouring out of the Spirit of God, which has been of late in this part of New England, of which we, in this town, have had such a share." But unlike most eschatologists, American or any other, Edwards believed that the millennium would come before the apocalypse. "Thus after such a happy and glorious season, such a long day of light and holiness, of love, and peace, and joy, now it shall again be a dark time."[58] Then the day of judgment would be at hand, the wicked punished, the elect gathered in, and the great work of redemption finished. Much as he had faithfully narrated the work in Northampton three years before, much as he would narrate an earlier work upon himself some months hence, Edwards narrated the redemptive work of God throughout all time, connecting at once past and place and person, and so, in a way, town and minister, to the grand design of history. "How rational, worthy, and excellent a revelation is this!," he concluded; "how excellent a book is the Bible, which contains so much beyond all other books in the world!" By year's end he would preach on the need to read that book and know it.

In "The Importance and Advantage of a thorough Knowledge of Divine Truth" (Heb. 5:12),[59] Edwards reminds his congregation that the Bible is both rational and spiritual, a source of speculative and practical knowledge and the path from the head to the heart. "Such is the nature of man, that nothing can come at the heart, but through the door of the understanding. And there can be no spiritual knowledge of that which there is not first a rational knowledge. . . . He cannot have a taste of sweetness and divine excellency of such and such things contained in divinity, unless he first have a notion that there are such and such things." As soldiers learn war and mariners the sea, so Christians should learn divinity, should study at "the school of Christ," should *"search"* the meaning of the Bible, because Scripture, "by the harmony of the different parts of it, casts great light upon itself."

It was the *History* once again and proof, if his congregation needed any, of a decade of orthodoxy, enlivened by surprising conversions and methods entirely new. "The things of divinity," Edwards pointed out in that November sermon, "not only concern ministers, but are of infinite importance to all Christians." As the next decade opened, his congregation, mindful of his words, shared those divine truths with him; by its close, still mindful, they denied him his truth and with it his pulpit.

Chapter Four
"Now, now, then is the time"

Among those gathered on New Haven common to hear his Yale commencement address in the late summer of 1741 were two divinity students, met, it must have seemed to Jonathan Edwards, in a special providence of God. By the end of the decade, Edwards would write an account of the life of David Brainerd, a sophomore then, that would become his most popular book in the nineteenth century, the one constant in a changing reputation. Samuel Hopkins became his disciple that day. A senior, he left New Haven for a two-year stay at the parsonage on King Street, becoming one of Edwards's New Divinity men, and, in 1765, his first biographer. But Edwards's fame waited on neither young man. The Yale invitation, unlike the Boston one ten years earlier, bore witness not to his promise but to its fulfillment, much as the invitation to preach at Enfield, Connecticut, in early July took the measure of it. Besides, the commencement marked another beginning. A year earlier, 14 September, George Whitefield landed in Newport, Rhode Island, to begin an American crusade that by mid-October would take him to Northampton and five exhortations in three days.

By 10 September 1741, then, the Great Awakening was abroad, and Edwards, sometime tutor and faithful narrator, returned to Yale to explain the "uncommon operation" of the spirit of God in New England and to defend it.[1] He could, of course, trace its history to the surprising conversions he recorded in the 1730s and to the "harvests" his grandfather had reaped many years before, but he chose instead to chart its symptoms, as he had in *A Divine and Supernatural Light* (1734) and in *Faithful Narrative* (1737); he called them *Distinguishing Marks* (1741). Over the next several years his interest in the conversion experience grew as the Great Awakening, and local satisfaction with it, waned. In *Some Thoughts* (1743) he turned back moderate and hostile criticism of it; in *Religious Affections* (1746) he numbered the twelve certain signs of it; in *Humble Attempt* (1747) he called for the worldwide prayer to promote it; and in *Humble Inquiry* (1749) he denied church membership without evidence of it. On the first day of summer

1750, his evangelical ministry came to an end. That evening Northampton voted overwhelmingly to dismiss him.

The Torments of Hell

Sinners. No one, least of all Edwards, saw that possibility in February 1740 when he framed "Man's natural Blindness in the Things of Religion" (Ps. 94:8–11), three sermons that chronicle assorted spiritual errors from animism to Arminianism. Errors of open profession, he argues, arise from ignorance and delusion: in Jews, Catholics, and Moslems, from a blindness to truth; in the learned of France, England, and America, from a blindness to faith. "And after this manner does this miserable world go on in endless confusion: like a great multitude of fool-hardy persons, who go on in the dark, stumbling and justling one against another, without perceiving any remedy for their own, or affording any for their neighbours' calamity." Other errors arise from the inward experiences or outward practices of would-be Christians, from their worldliness and their sins, from their self-interest and their short-sightedness. In the application, Edwards urges the light of Christ on natural man whose fall from grace has dimmed his understanding. Only in an outpouring of God's spirit and in the *"plain preaching"* of Scripture can sight be restored to the blind and wisdom to the ignorant.[2]

In two sermons in June, "Hypocrites deficient in the Duty of Prayer" (Job 27:10), Edwards turns to the "common illumination" of the false convert and the light that darkens as the fires of hell recede. He warns against inconstancy and remembers the backsliding of another time. "When the business and cares of the world shall again begin to crowd a little upon you, or the next time you shall go out into young company, it is probable you will again neglect this duty. The next time a *frolic* shall be appointed, to which it is proposed to you to go, it is highly probable you will neglect not only secret prayer, but also family prayer."[3] The following month he preaches upon the business of the world in "The Sin of Theft and of Injustice" (Ex. 20:15, "Thou shalt not steal"), a caution to the river merchants ranged in proper rows before him.[4] Less "practical" is a September sermon, "The Manner in which the Salvation of the Soul is to be sought" (Gen. 6:22), an exercise in the typology of Noah's ark. Edwards considers the "business" of building salvation a "great *labour* and *care*," a daily business of *"great expense,"* a distressful and troublesome venture "in need of coun-

sel," a business that "never ends till *life* ends." In the second half of
the sermon, the metaphor shifts to the "boisterous waves" of the
flood—"an image of that terrible out-pouring of the wrath of God"—
and the billows of destruction, likened to the "vast liquid mountains
of fire" in hell.[5]

By December the fires are no longer the "vast waves" or billows of
an anti-type but the "devouring" ones of the refining crucible and the
glassblower's furnace, the fires of "The Fearfulness, which will hereafter surprise Sinners in Zion" (Isa. 33:14). In such heat the wicked
shall know their torment with a "quick sense within and without; their
heads, their eyes, their tongues, their hands, their feet, their loins,
and their vitals, shall for ever be full of glowing melting fire, fierce
enough to melt the very rocks and elements" in an eternity that "swallows up all thought and imagination." Earlier Edwards sketched a
death-bed scene—the "countenance" of the physician, "a whispering
in the room," the "cold deathsweat," "nature dissolving," the soul
"agoing"—and the inexpressible terror of the unrepentant. "What, in
such a case, is left in the soul, in those last moments, when it is just
breaking its bonds with the body, about to fetch its leap, and is on the
edge of eternity, and the very brink of hell, without any Saviour, or
the least testimony of divine mercy: I say, what is sometimes felt by
Christless souls in these moments, none can tell; nor is it within the
compass of our conception." At the end of the sermon he brings the
terrors of his graphic hell to the meetinghouse itself. "It is an awful
thing to think of, that there are now some persons in this very congregation, here and there, in one seat or another, who will be the subjects
of that very misery of which we have now heard, although it be so
dreadful, although it be so intolerable, and although it be eternal!"
But God has come again to Northampton, the "same great God who
so wonderfully appeared" six years ago, bringing hope of salvation.
"Now, now, then, is the time; now is the blessed opportunity to escape
those everlasting burnings." Now, Edwards promises, an awakening is
at hand.[6]

In the same month, December, he preached on "The Portion of the
Righteous" (Rom. 2:10), about the happiness of the redeemed; the
loveliness of Christ, "without spot or wrinkle"; and the sweetness of
the soul, a flower "open before the sun to be filled with his light and
pleasant influences!" The landscape of heaven is as splendid in its way
as hell is horrific, and just as inexpressible, "what we cannot conceive
of," what John in Revelation can only hint at.[7] But by April Edwards

leaves the "perfect state" of man to resume his old imprecations, meting out a portion to the damned in "The future Punishment of the Wicked unavoidable and intolerable," two sermons based on Ezek. 22:14, "Can thine heart endure, or can thine hands be strong, in the days that I shall deal with thee?" In that question Edwards finds the substance of his indictment and its controlling image.[8]

In the hands. Other images occur, images of debt and rebellion—God exacting "the very uttermost farthing" in the business of judgment; men of "demure countenance" and "rebellious hearts" carrying "their swords under their skirts"—and images of the tallying fires of hell:

[I]magine yourself to be cast into a fiery oven, all of a glowing heat, or into the midst of a glowing brickkiln, or of a great furnace, where your pain would be as much greater than that occasioned by accidentally touching a coal of fire, as the heat is greater. Imagine also that your body were to lie there for a quarter of an hour, full of fire, as full within and without as a bright coal of fire, all the while full of quick sense; what horror would you feel at the entrance of such a furnace! And how long would that quarter of an hour seem to you! If it were to be measured by a glass, how long would the glass seem to be running! And after you had endured it for one minute, how overbearing would it be to you to think that you had it to endure the other fourteen!

And how would you endure twenty-four hours, a year, a thousand years, "millions of millions of ages," and "never, never" to be delivered!

But the image of hands, the hands of sinners, of God, even of Edwards "handling" the doctrine, shapes this sermon, concentrating its energy. "It is with our hands that we make and accomplish things for ourselves," but we have not "the strength of hand" to bring about our own deliverance nor to stay "the hands of the great God." Sinners are "nothing, and less than nothing in the hands of an angry God." They should surrender themselves—"Thine hands would drop down at once"—to the divine judgment as "God takes the matter into his own hands." Imagine "what a poor hand you would make" fighting the fires of hell. "You have often seen a spider, or some other noisome insect, when thrown in the midst of a fierce fire. . . . There is no long struggle, no fighting against the fire, no strength exerted to oppose the heat, or to fly from it; but it immediately stretches forth itself and yields; and the fire takes possession of it, and at once it becomes full of fire." Impenitent sinners cannot avoid their punishment by the strength of their own hands, cannot escape, cannot find relief with "so much as a drop of water to cool their tongues," cannot bear their eternal torment. "You who now hear of hell and the wrath of the great God, and sit here in these seats so easy and quiet, and go away so careless; by and by will shake, and tremble, and cry out, and shriek, and gnash your teeth, and will be thoroughly convinced of the vast weight and importance of these things, which you now despise." Two months later, another imprecatory sermon burns through central Connecticut—and the American imagination—with images of hands and hell and spiders.

Sinners in the Hands of an Angry God, delivered at Enfield on 8 July 1741, in a quietly dispassionate voice and "At a Time of great Awakenings," was "attended with remarkable Impressions of many of the Hearers," as the title page went on to say, the shakes and shrieks Edwards had promised in April.[9] Published later that year in Boston and a dozen more times over the next hundred years, including once in Choctaw for the Cherokee Nation, the twenty-five-page sermon is often reprinted and excerpted, and perhaps now stands Edwards's best known work and for many readers, unfortunately, his only one. The text, Deut. 32:35, "Their foot shall slide in due time," was one he had used three times before, most recently in Northampton in June. The doctrine, "'There is nothing that keeps wicked men at any moment out of hell, but the mere pleasure of God,'" was the orthodox one of the utter dependence of man—the righteous and wicked alike—upon the sovereign and arbitrary will of God, a view Edwards shared with his Boston audience in *God Glorified* ten years ago to the day.

The Enfield sermon gathers its arguments on natural man's dependence in ten short "considerations" following the doctrine: 1) God has the power to cast sinners into hell; 2) they deserve it as divine justice; 3) they are already under condemnation of the law; 4) they are objects of God's wrath; 5) Satan stands ready to seize them; 6) they are controlled by hellish principles; 7) they are not secure; 8) their wisdom will not help them; 9) they cannot contrive an escape; and 10) God is under no obligation to keep them from hell, except as they believe in Christ. Images fully developed in "Future Punishment" are tempered here, are somewhat less compelling. "Men's hands cannot be strong when God rises up. The strongest have no power to resist him, nor can any deliver out of his hands. . . . Though hand join in hand, and vast multitudes of God's enemies combine and associate themselves, they are easily broken in pieces." The sword of rebellion, tucked "under their skirts" in the earlier sermon, becomes the sword of divine retribution restrained, "every moment brandished over their heads, and it is nothing but the hand of arbitrary mercy, and God's mere will, that holds it back." Hell, the very expression of divine wrath, "is prepared; the fire is made ready; the furnace is now hot; the flames do now rage and glow." Yet its geography remains vague. Even figures derived from the text—"he that stands or walks on slippery ground needs nothing but his own weight to throw him down"—seem less eternal, more down-home. "Unconverted men walk over the pit of hell on a rotten covering, and there are innumerable places in this covering so weak that they will not bear their weight, and these places are not seen."[10]

Of an angry God. If, then, the text and the doctrine seem pageworn and the tropes familiar and tame, the application—fully half the length of the sermon—does not. It begins, commonly enough, with a shift in the point of view. "The use may be of awakening to unconverted persons in this congregation. This that you have heard is the case of every one of you that are out of Christ." But when the application turns to illustration, the rhetoric takes on a fresh terror, second-person rural. "There are the black clouds of God's wrath now hanging directly over your heads, full of the dreadful storm, and big with thunder; and were it not for the restraining hand of God, it would immediately burst forth upon you. The sovereign pleasure of God, for the present, stays his rough wind; otherwise it would come with fury, and your destruction would come like a whirlwind, and you would be like the chaff of the summer threshing floor." The wrath of God is likened to dammed waters "continually rising," His hand staying the floodgate; or it is likened to a bent bow, "the arrow made ready on the string," only the "mere pleasure of God, and that an angry God, without any promise or obligation at all, that keeps the arrow one moment from being made drunk with your blood."[11]

Earlier in the sermon Edwards wrote of "natural men . . . held in the hand of God, over the pit of hell," flames flashing about them, the fire within "struggling to break out," their safety preserved one moment to the next by "the mere arbitrary will, and uncovenanted, unobliged forbearance of an incensed God." Now, in the application, Edwards repeats the scene, but man is metamorphized into the spider of boyhood memory and God is transfixed in hate.

The God that holds you over the pit of hell, much as one holds a spider, or some loathsome insect, over the fire, abhors you, and is dreadfully provoked;

his wrath towards you burns like fire; he looks upon you as worthy of nothing else, but to be cast into the fire; he is of purer eyes than to bear to have you in his sight; you are ten thousand times more abominable in his eyes, as the most hateful venomous serpent is in ours. You have offended him infinitely more than ever a stubborn rebel did his prince. And yet it is nothing but his hand that holds you from falling into the fire every moment. It is to be ascribed to nothing else, that you did not go to hell the last night; that you was suffered to awake again in this world, after you closed your eyes to sleep. And there is no other reason to be given, why you have not dropped into hell since you arose in the morning, but that God's hand has held you up. There is no other reason to be given why you have not gone to hell, since you have sat here in the house of God, provoking his pure eyes by your sinful wicked manner of attending his solemn worship. Yea, there is nothing else that is to be given as a reason why you do not this very moment drop down into hell.[12]

Earlier in the sermon Edwards noted that men find it easy "to cut or singe a slender thread that any thing hangs by"; now he cries, "O sinner!," like the spider itself, "You hang by a slender thread, with the flames of divine wrath flashing about it, and ready every moment to singe it, and burn it asunder." The shift from active agent to passive, from country fact to figure underscores Enfield's dependence and its terrifying insecurity. The spider of certain punishment in April hangs now—depends—on a filament of hope.

"Christ has flung the door of mercy wide open," inviting young and old to be born again, "however moral and strict, sober and religious, they may otherwise be." The infinitely fierce divine sovereign stays his hand this Sunday morning. "How awful it is to be left behind at such a day!"

If we knew that there was one person, and but one, in the whole congregation, that was to be the subject of this misery, what an awful thing it would be to think of! If we knew who it was, what an awful sight would it be to see such a person! How might all the rest of the congregation lift up a lamentable and bitter cry over him! But, alas! instead of one, how many is it likely will remember this discourse in hell! And it would be a wonder, if some that are now present should not be in hell in a very short time, even before this year is out. And it would be no wonder if some persons, that now sit here, in some seats of this meeting-house, in health, quiet and secure, should be there before to-morrow morning.[13]

"[Y]our damnation does not slumber," Edwards warns. Now, now is the time to awake. "'There was such a breathing of distress, and weep-

ing,'" a visiting minister reports, "'that the preacher was obliged to
speak to the people and desire silence, that he might be heard.'"[14] Two
months later, New Haven, dry-eyed and critical, heard him out in
silence.

On Alien Ground

Extraordinary circumstances. Eight days before his Yale appearance, Edwards delivered the funeral sermon for his uncle, the Reverend William Williams of Hatfield. The first of his three eulogies to
be published—the others were for Col. John Stoddard and David
Brainerd—*Resort and Remedy* (Matt. 14:12) is, expectedly, full of praise
and sympathy. "God has now taken away from you an able and faithful
minister of the New Testament, one that had long been a FATHER to
you, and a FATHER in our Israel, a person of uncommon natural abil-
ities, comprehensive knowledge, and of a solid, accurate judgment."
Buried with him for a time apparently was some of the bitterness of
the Williams clan, which dated back to Edwards's undergraduate days
at Yale. It had cropped up again in 1736.

Benjamin Colman had added a shortened *Faithful Narrative* to a pair
of sermons of the seventy-year-old Williams and published the whole
of it without permission of either uncle or nephew. That the complete
narrative was first published abroad rather than in Boston may be due
to the influence of the Williamses upon local publishing houses; that
they were later active in Edwards's dismissal from Northampton and
in his troubles in Stockbridge is beyond question. Nevertheless, *Resort
and Remedy* was published "at the united Request of those Reverend
and Honoured Gentlemen, the Sons of the Deceased," and Edwards
took the opportunity to forward his cause and concern. Like him, Williams was "eminently an evangelical preacher," who "for so long a time
continued to exhort you," though "obstinately some of you slighted
his counsels," and whom you may see "sitting with Christ to judge
and condemn you, and adoring his awful justice on your aggravated
punishment," an application that reads eerily like Edwards's *Farewell
Sermon.*[15]

Little more than a week later he was in New Haven lecturing not
only on the "evangelical subjects" of his late uncle's "delight" but on
the "agonies of body," the very "tears, trembling, groans, loud out-
cries" he had aroused and then tried to still at Enfield. The full title
of the Yale address states the matter in brief: *The Distinguishing Marks
Of a Work of the Spirit of God. Applied to that uncommon Operation that has*

*lately appeared on the Minds of many of the People of this Land: With a
particular Consideration of the extraordinary Circumstances with which this
Work is attended* (1741).[16] The text, 1 John 4:1, or rather "the chapter
wherein is the text," limits the subject to scriptural evidences. And a
familiar figure, early in the argument, sets the tone:

If we should suppose that a person saw himself hanging over a great pit, full
of fierce and glowing flames, by a thread that he knew to be very weak, and
not sufficient long to bear his weight, and knew that multitudes had been in
such circumstances before, and that most of them had fallen and perished;
and saw nothing within reach, that he could take hold of to save him; what
distress would he be in? How ready to think that *now* the thread is breaking;
now, this minute, he should be swallowed up in these dreadful flames? And
would not he be ready to cry out in such circumstances? How much more
those that see themselves in this manner hanging over an infinitely more
dreadful pit, or held over it in the hand of God, who at the same time they
see to be exceedingly provoked? No wonder they are ready to expect every
moment when this angry God will let them drop; and no wonder they cry out
of their misery; and no wonder that the wrath of God when manifested but a
little to the soul, overbears human strength.[17]

Although Edwards defends imprecatory sermons in the course of his
address, his language here lacks the fire and pain of the Northampton
sermons and the awful promises made at Enfield. It is analytical and
measured throughout, cool almost. The occasion was different, of
course, even if the times were not, and he brought assurances and his
quiet presence to New Haven, restive after the itinerant preacher James
Davenport, another son of Yale, had provoked both ministers and people to outrage just days before. The Great Awakening is a work of God,
Edwards explained; to judge it by its excesses is both illogical and
unscriptural. "Beloved," his text began, "believe not every spirit, but
try the spirits whether they be of God; because many false prophets are
gone out into the world."

Negative signs and positive. The structure of *Distinguishing
Marks* follows that of *A Divine and Supernatural Light*: first, things that
are not, then, things that are. First, nine negative instances, "what are
not signs that we are to judge a work by, whether it be the work of
the Spirit of God or no"; then, five positive signs, "what are the sure,
distinguishing, Scripture evidences and marks of a work of the Spirit
of God."[18] The order of the positive signs derives from the sequence
found in 1 John 14; the order of the negative signs moves from the

general to the specific. The application, like that in *Sinners in the Hands of an Angry God,* takes up more than half the volume and is divided into three parts. The peroration calls on the "zealous friends" of the Awakening to avoid the show of "an angry zeal" in contending with opponents of the revival—as he has this very day, he might have added.

In the first of his nine negative signs, Edwards maintains that an extraordinary event testifies neither to its truth nor its falsity. That the minds of "very many," especially the "very young," may be "strangely affected," may be "moved with very extraordinary affections of fear, sorrow, desire, love or joy," and may be altered in their "frames," proves nothing: "these things are no argument that the work is not a work of the spirit of God." Indeed, "God has still new things to accomplish," especially in the latter days, so that the past may be no clue to the present. Nor are bodily effects, the subject of the second sign, a clue. These cannot be judged "one way or the other, . . . because the Scripture nowhere gives us any such rule," though it is altogether reasonable to suppose that, given human nature, any calamity—war, let's say, or the threat of it—induces strange, untoward effects in people. No more is the "great deal of noise about religion" now current an indication of how matters stand, even though it would be "a great absurdity," Edwards notes in the third sign, to think that a work of God would not stir "open commotion." He reminds his audience in the fourth sign that those who have imaginative impressions "don't prove that they have nothing else"; it is, after all, human nature and the working of the mind. "I have been acquainted with some such instances" of a "kind of ecstasy" or vision of being "wrapped up even to heaven." It may be that "persons under a true sense of the glorious and wonderful greatness and excellency of divine things, and soul-ravishing views of the beauty and love of Christ, should have the strength of nature overpowered," much as he recorded the experiences of others in *Faithful Narrative* and his own a few years later. That such experiences serve as examples is both scriptural—"God's manner"—and reasonable, according to the fifth sign. "'Tis no argument that men are not influenced by reason, that they are influenced by example." Or, more broadly, "There is a language in actions; and in some cases, much more clear and convincing than in words." For Edwards, John Locke had become an empiricism of the Word.

The remaining four negative signs concern either errors of judgment or excesses of conduct. The sixth sign takes up the problem of "great imprudences and irregularities" of some of the affected, which Edwards dismisses in the second sentence: "We are to consider that the end for which God pours out his Spirit, is to make men holy, and not to make them politicians." From the time of the apostles to the reformation of Calvin there have been "notable" instances of irregularity, "running out some way or other into an undue severity," a history of intolerance and persecution. Errors of judgment or "delusions of Satan" are no proof against a true work of God, he remarks in the seventh sign, because for a while "the new man and the old man subsist together in the same person." Even "gross errors or scandalous practices" do not prove a work false, he adds in the eighth sign. "If we look into church history," from the Gnostics to the Anabaptists, we read tales of "whimsical and extravagant errors, and gross enthusiasm, boasting of high degrees of spirituality and perfection, censuring and condemning others as carnal." So, too, "in the beginning of New England, in her purest days, when vital piety flourished, such kind of things as these broke out." In the last sign, Edwards turns to more recent history—New Haven a few days ago; Enfield two months ago—and to ministers who insist "very much on the terrors of God's holy law, and that with a great deal of pathos and earnestness." Imprecatory sermons are "the best kindness," he asserts, the crying aloud to a child in a burning house. Like the fifth sign, it is simply a matter of joining words to acts: "if we look on language as a communication of our minds to others," then the language of a minister's actions is "much more effectual than the bare signification of his words," though "indecent boisterousness" is unnatural and should be avoided. "Some talk of it as an unreasonable thing to think to fright persons to heaven; but I think it is a reasonable thing to endeavor to fright persons away from hell." Some at Yale thought that such reasonableness smacked of danger.

The five positive signs have little to do with reason or with possibilities: they are scriptural, clear, and certain, the "sure" signs. When a spirit raises the "esteem and respect" of a people for Christ; operates upon them against Satan "of this world"; moves them to a "greater regard" for the Bible; leads them to "those things that are true" in revelation; and brings them to love God and man—that is the unmistakable spirit of God at work upon the land. "These marks, that the Apostle [John] has given us, are sufficient to stand alone, and support themselves; and wherever they may be, they plainly show the finger of God, and are sufficient to outweigh a thousand such little objections, as many make from oddities, irregularities, and errors in conduct, and the delusions and scandals of some professors."

The unsearchable heart. By such signs or "rules," Edwards insists in the three-part application, the Great Awakening is "undoubtedly, in the general," a work of the spirit of God. And its "notorious" facts, known to everyone everywhere "(unless it be some that have been very much out of the way of observing and hearing indeed)," just confirm it. So widespread are the physical manifestations of the current revival that few could "put a cheat upon others," as Edwards can testify: "among the many hundreds, and it may be thousands, that have lately been brought to such agonies, I never yet knew one, lastingly deprived of their reason." The work is a true work of the spirit of God even if a bit awkward for dimity souls.

Not but that I think that persons that are thus extraordinarily moved should endeavor to refrain from outward manifestations, what they well can, and should refrain to their utmost, in the time of the solemn worship. But if God is pleased to convince the consciences of persons, so that they can't avoid great outward manifestations, even to the interrupting and breaking off those public means they were attending, I don't think this is confusion, or an unhappy interruption, any more than if a company should meet on the field to pray for rain, and should be broken off from their exercise by a plentiful shower. [19]

He recalls the "happiness" of his Northampton settlement and the work God wrought there over the years, his grandfather's harvests and his own, adding that the current revival has been "much purer" than that of six years ago.

In the second part of the application, Edwards warns opposers of the revival in New England not to "clog" the work of God nor "speak contemptibly" of it, lest they be guilty of the "unpardonable sin against the Holy Ghost." In the third part, [20] he advises friends and promoters of the revival "to avoid all errors and misconduct," to act with humility and charity—he explicates 1 Cor. 13, the text of *Charity and Its Fruits*—and to be wary of inspiration: "I know that they that leave the sure word of prophecy, that God has given us to be a light shining in a dark place, to follow impressions and impulses, leave the guidance of the pole star to follow a Jack-with-a-lanthorn." He argues for a trained ministry—"let us not despise human learning"—though some may "speak profitably, yea, very excellently, without study." He pleads for an end to the judgment and censure of one professing Christian by another, accounting it God's prerogative to judge, not man's, and not his, certainly. "I know by experience that there is a great aptness in men, that think they have had some experience of the power of religion, to think themselves sufficient to discern and determine the state of others' souls by a little conversation with them; and experience has taught me that 'tis an error. I once did not imagine that the heart of man had been so unsearchable as I find it is." Still, he would search it out over the next several years in signs of religious affections and qualifications for communion. In the meantime, he would continue to write of the revival as he had, "very free from an enthusiastic or a party spirit," as William Cooper put it.

Some Thoughts on the Great Awakening

Seasonable errors.   Yale, apparently, thought otherwise, and in a short time she abandoned him and his party, the liberal, sometimes burning, New Lights of evangelism. *Some Thoughts,* his 378-page defense of the Great Awakening in March 1743, only widened the breach, and the conservative, often cold, Old Lights of rationalism turned against him. Within six months of its publication, the Reverend Dr. Charles Chauncy of the Old Brick Church, Boston, judged much of the revival a fraud and Edwards a guilty apologist in the even longer *Seasonable Thoughts on the State of Religion in New England: A Treatise in Five Parts* (1743), a part-by-part, often page-by-page, rebuttal of Edwards's evidence.[21] New or old, the lights were going out on the revival all over New England.

Some Thoughts Concerning the present Revival of Religion In New-England, And the Way in which it ought to be acknowledged and promoted (1743) continues Edwards's argument for the revival in much the same pattern as the Yale address, showing in turn how promoters of the work have been "injuriously blamed" and how "positively" to combat that.[22] For his part, Edwards promises to speak freely about the "important war" of conversion—"In a free nation, such liberty of the press is allowed"— and to put an end to the "sad janglings and confusion" attending it. In the first part he explains that the Great Awakening is indeed a "glorious" work of God.

Three errors of judgment underline the "ill thoughts" of those who question the legitimacy of the revival, logical errors and scriptural ones. First, it is an error to judge a work a priori, especially as God begins at the "lower end," using the weak and foolish, the young and the infirm, people and ministers alike. Second, it is an error to consider either philosophy or history the criterion of judgment. Scripture, not

philosophy, describes the nature of the soul, and holy affection—
equated here with the will—is the "very life" of true religion, a matter
not of the head but of the heart, often raised to "an exceeding great
height" of passion. "Things of religion take place in men's hearts," he
writes at about the time he is composing the lectures that will become
Religious Affections. "The informing of the understanding is all in vain,
any farther than it affects the heart." Scripture concerns the moral state
of men, "not physic and anatomy," and it gives ministers rules enough
to judge spiritual health. Bodily effects such as pulse rates, pallor,
tears, trembling, and convulsions are left unremarked in the Bible and
are, therefore, irrelevant. Besides, "so very few" out of so very many
have behaved badly, certainly "not enough to cause us to be in any
fright, . . . unless we are disposed to gather up all that we can to
darken it, and set it forth in frightful colors." Nor can history be a
guide. Edwards counters charges of untested newness with citations
from earlier published accounts of remarkable conversions here and
abroad and with a recent letter from his aging father testifying to "what
he remembers formerly to have heard." Third, it is an error to judge
"all in a lump," the good and bad indiscriminately; it is a logical fallacy
to judge the whole by a part or an essential effect by an occasional
cause. "As after nature has long been shut up in a cold dead state, in
time of winter, when the sun returns in the spring, there is, together
with the increase of light and heat of the sun, very dirty and tempes-
tuous weather, before all is settled calm and serene, and all nature
rejoices in its bloom and beauty," so natural man suffers a "common
corruption" before he rejoices in Christ. And so the people of New
England have changed remarkably over the last year or two, despite
"imprudences" and "sinful irregularities," despite "transports and ecstasies," "faintings, and agitations of the body." Especially the young
among them, but as well "great beaus and fine ladies," "poor Indians"
and "poor Negroes," even the "most sober and pious," have brought a
"strange alteration" to their ways and a "sensible, strong and sweet
love to God." "Is it not a shame to New England," he asks, "that such
a work should be much doubted here?"

An uncommon narrative.   In answer, Edwards wrote of the
"high and extraordinary transports" of a person he has been "particularly acquainted with," an account of some twenty pages in the first
edition, often in "the person's own expressions," yet nothing more specific than that—not even a pronoun—to tell that it was the personal
narrative of his wife Sarah.[23] He left her and his pulpit for a round of

sermons and lectures in nearby Leicester in late January 1742, entrusting the care of his flock and family to the young Samuel Buell, like Hopkins, a graduating senior at the last September's commencement. When he returned a fortnight later he found Northampton "in a great and continual commotion, day and night" and Sarah "swallowed up with light and love and a sweet solace, rest and joy of soul, that was altogether unspeakable." He told of the "very great effects" on her body,

sometimes the hands clinched, and the flesh cold, but senses still remaining; animal nature often in a great emotion and agitation, and the soul very often, of late, so overcome with great admiration, and a kind of omnipotent joy, as to cause the person (wholly unavoidably) to leap with all the might, with joy and mighty exultation of soul; the soul at the same time being so strongly drawn towards God and Christ in heaven, that it seemed to the person as though soul and body would, as it were of themselves, of necessity mount up, leave the earth and ascend thither.

Edwards traces her agitation and delights to 1734–35—the Abigail Hutchinson and Phebe Bartlet years—and notes that they increased "greatly" in 1739, "a very dead time." "They arose," he adds pointedly, "from no distemper catched from Mr. Whitefield or Mr. Tennent, because they began before either of them came into the country," nor from "that enthusiastical town of Northampton (as some may be ready to call it)," because she was raised elsewhere and converted many years before. Though she had suffered "many ups and downs," bouts of melancholy, and "a vapoury habit of body" in earlier, less gracious times, she became "a new person," living in an "overwhelming" clearness of divine light and in an "altogether overpowering" sweetness of divine love, in charity, judging not, imbued with "a new sense" of moral social duties and "an extraordinary sense of the awful majesty and greatness of God," "longing, as the person expressed it, to sit and sing this life away." With words like these before him, recalling as they do his youthful account of Sarah in New Haven and the narrative of his own conversion sometime later, Edwards cries out, "Now if such things are enthusiasm, and the fruits of a distempered brain, let my brain be evermore possessed of that happy distemper! If this be distraction, I pray God that the world of mankind may be all seized with this benign, meek, beneficient, beatifical, glorious distraction!" What, he asks, are the doubters of the revival waiting for? To him it is "evident" that the revival is "a very great and wonderful, and exceeding glorious work of God," one "vastly beyond any former outpouring of the Spirit that ever was known in New England."

In Part II, Edwards considers "the obligations that all are under to acknowledge, rejoice in, and promote" the revival, and he cautions against indecisiveness. "At a time when God manifests himself in such a great work for his church, there is no such things as being neuters." He interrupts a catalogue of examples and warnings from the Bible about the work of God in order to locate its end. The millennium, Edwards contends, will probably begin in America, as Isa. 60:9 suggests: "I can't think that anything else can be here intended but America by 'the isles that are far off.'" That the biblical "new" world was discovered at about the time of the Reformation; that it was a wilderness, "dry sand and barren rocks," upon which God would build a paradise; that the "Sun of righteousness has long been going down from East to West"—all these mark America as the probable site of the millennium. "And if we may suppose that his glorious work of God shall begin in any part of America, I think, if we consider the circumstances of the settlement of New England, it must needs appear the most likely of all American colonies, to be the place whence this work shall principally take its rise."[24] The Great Awakening is but the "dawn" to that day, he reminds his readers, as he has "long insisted upon this point." After his foray into eschatology, Edwards returns to his catalogue of scriptural texts about a manifest work of God, citing a dozen to the page at times, and warns "all sorts of persons in New England" to "take great notice of his [God's] hand in this mighty work of grace," to acknowledge and promote it, rulers and ministers and people, especially "the press."

Subtle enemies and fervent friends. The next two parts of *Some Thoughts* are given over to a defense of the active promoters of the revival, the injuries they have been made to suffer at the hands of "subtle and cruel enemies," and the errors they may have fallen into in their zeal. In Part III, Edwards answers ten charges made "without, or beyond, just cause" by the enemies of the revival, countering criticism with pastoral experience and scriptural example. To the charge that ministers address the emotions rather than the understanding, he offers the rhetoric of religious affections: "Our people don't so much need to have their heads stored, as to have their hearts touched"; to the charge that ministers preach unwonted terror, he offers the simple arithmetic of salvation; to the charge that they frighten children, the need to "deal plainly" with the "young vipers"; that people exchange religious meetings for temporal duties, gain instead of loss: "more time has been saved from frolicking and tavern-haunting, idleness, unprofitable visits, vain talk, fruitless pastimes, and needless diversions"; that frequent sermons overwhelm and confuse an auditory, a theory of timely impressions; that ministers accept bodily effects as "probably tokens of God's presence," the evidence of particular experiences; that "strongly seized" persons adversely affect a congregation, the "happy influence" of example, "which is often spoken of in Scripture as one of the chief means by which God would carry on his work, in the time of the prosperity of religion in the latter days"; that people talk endlessly and passionately "with such earnestness and vehemence," the intoxicating wine of the Word; that they sing overmuch the psalms of David or the hymns of Watts, the consequence of their joy: "I can see no reason why we should limit ourselves to such particular forms of words that we find in the Bible, in speaking to him by way of praise, in meter, and with music, than when we speak to him in prose, by way of prayer and supplication"; and that children convene in prayer, the converting ways of their elders. Such unmerited charges at an end, the argument shifts to what Edwards regards as more justifiable criticism, the excesses of overzealous promoters of the revival.

Part IV, the longest section of his defense—it runs to a third of the text—focusses on but three causes of error: spiritual pride, wrong principles, and ignorance of Satan's advantages. For each, Edwards exacts a complex of reasons and actions, and to each he tenders a modest remedy as a "hearty and fervent friend" of the revival. Spiritual pride encompasses the heart like "the coats of an onion; if you pull off one there is another underneath." The true Christian, on the other hand, is humble, "clothed all over" in meekness and mildness, in a "gentleness of spirit" and a "winning air." People and ministers, "above all" itinerant preachers, should avoid roughness, boldness, and contentiousness. "Indeed to spend a great deal of time in jangling and warm debates about religion, is not to propagate religion, but to hinder it."

Among seven wrong principles, the second source of error, Edwards lists inspiration of immediate revelation—the Bible would be rendered "in a great measure useless"—, errors in logic, attestations of divine providence, a disregard for the order and outward forms of religion, and the ordination of an unlearned ministry. "The opening a door for the admission of unlearned men to the work of the ministry, though they should be persons of extraordinary experience, would on some accounts be especially prejudicial at such a day as this" because lacking "an extensive knowledge," they might lead the susceptible to "impulses, vain imaginations, superstition, indiscreet zeal, and such like extremes."

The final cause for error, the ignorance of Satan's special advantage, derives, first, from the inward experiences of Christians, such that true grace may be mixed with false or brotherly love with lust, and second, from the outward effects of those experiences, which for the good of the revival should be held under "gentle restraint." To this Edwards adds two particularly troublesome errors (and their effects) that arise from one or another of the three major causes, censuring church members as unconverted or unqualified—a "bitter root" that "must be totally rooted out"—and exhorting by the laity. "No man but only a minister that is duly appointed to that sacred calling ought to follow teaching and exhorting as a calling, or so as to neglect that which is his proper calling." Finally, Edwards urges a return to decorum in church—a "moderate restraint" on the noise at services and an imperative to silence at communion—though he finds no "valid objection" to singing God's praises on the way there. Thus, he concludes, many things "amiss" in the revival have hampered its success, otherwise "this work would have so prevailed as before this time to have carried all afore it, and have triumphed over New England as its conquest." And so the last, the fifth part of *Some Thoughts,* will show "positively what ought to be done" to bring that about.

There are "faults on both sides," Edwards begins, "mixtures of light and dark"; there are "stumbling blocks" to be removed and "mutual forbearance" to be practiced; and there are, as in a sermon, improvements to be made. Orthodoxy ought to be reaffirmed and Arminian principles relinquished; the older generation ought to follow the younger in belief; ministers ought to seek grace, zeal, and resolution instead of "spending away their time in sitting and smoking, and in diverting, or worldly, unprofitable conversation, telling news, and making their remarks on this and the other trifling subject"; colleges ought to be "nurseries of piety," not wards of vice; the rich ought to use their wealth and power to further the revival, for scholarships, libraries, and schools for the Christian poor; all ought to honor God with days of fasting and unions of prayer: "all God's people in America . . . should all unite on the same day in humbling ourselves before God"; all ought to honor Him with more frequent communions, with the moral duties of love and charity, with a renewal of the covenant, and with the monthly publication of a history of His work.[25] Now, Edwards ends, God has given New England a "most happy season" to begin.

The Nature of True Religion

Purses and shining lights. Sometime between March and September 1743, between his defense of the Great Awakening and Chauncy's attack upon it, Edwards probably completed the cycle of lectures on religious affections that he began the year before, but another three years would pass before he had it ready for the press. By then the revival was spent, and Northampton fell to quarreling with him about fixed salaries, bad books, and admission policies. The questions that had "long engaged" him seemed to many an impertinence. "What," he had asked in the preface to *Religious Affections,* "is the nature of true religion?" By 1746, few in the Valley would stay for his answer.

Between times he published three sermons and three letters on the role of ministers, observations at once pastoral and personal. On 8 June 1743, in his ordination sermon for Jonathan Judd on Heb. 13:17, *Great Concern* (1743), he speaks of the "precious treasure" of souls he is about to "resign" to Judd's care and, prompted no doubt by recent events in town, the matter of money and "anti-ministerial men." "And here let me warn you in particular, that you do not only do pretty well by your minister for a while at first, while the relation between you is a new thing, and then afterward, when your minister's necessities are increased, begin to fail, as it too frequently happens."[26] Throughout much of another ordination sermon, *True Excellency* (1744)—this for Robert Abercrombie of nearby Pelham on 30 August 1744—Edwards elaborates upon the metaphor of his text, John 5:35, "He was a burning and a shining light," and achieves some striking figures.

When there is a light in a minister, consisting of human learning, great speculative knowledge and the wisdom of this world, without a spiritual warmth and ardor in his heart, and a holy zeal in his ministrations, his light is like the light of an *ignis fatuus,* and some kind of putrifying carcases that shine in the dark, though they are of a stinking savor. And if on the other hand a minister has warmth and zeal, without light, his heat has nothing excellent in it, but is rather to be abhorred; being like the heat of a bottomless pit; where, though the fire be great, yet there is no light. To be hot in this manner, and not lightsome, is to be like an angel of darkness.

Paying ministers, no less than defining them, Edwards adds, calls for light: "do not take a course to obscure and extinguish the light that would shine among you, and to smother and suppress the flame, by casting dirt upon it; by necessitating your minister by your penurious-ness towards him, to be involved in worldly care."[27] And, on 19 September 1746, at the installation of Samuel Buell—Sarah's late comforter—as pastor of East Hampton, Long Island, Edwards cele-brates in tropes *The Church's Marriage* (1746) of Isa. 62:4,5, pausing long enough to remind those assembled to "spare no pains nor cost" to keep their minister from "pinching necessities."[28]

Edwards's three letters tell another tale. Published as two pamphlets in 1745,[29] they recount—and vehemently deny—Rev. Thomas Clap's published allegation that on a journey to Boston Edwards revealed to him George Whitefield's scheme for "turning out the Generality of the Ministers in the Country" for proper, that is, converted, evangelicals from Britain and Ireland. That the rector of Yale could be "driven to great Straits," as Edwards put it, made clearer still the distrust official New Haven had for the Great Awakening and its intellectual avatar. Nothing, not even a 343-page dissertation on the psychology of reli-gion, would shake that.

Gracious operations and affections.   A *Treatise Concerning Re-ligious Affections* (1746), published just once during his life, became in time his most popular work, rivalling his *Life of Brainerd* in the nine-teenth century, and all but exceeding it in the twentieth, a practical handbook for evangelicals.[30] Edwards had, of course, written about holy affections before, most recently in *Some Thoughts,* where he claimed them to be "the very life and soul of all true religion" and where he connected them to the fruits of the revival. "What is [it] that any have a notion of, that is very sweet, excellent and joyful, of a religious nature, that is entirely of a different nature from these things?" At East Windsor and at Northampton, he had observed the work of the affections close at hand—"a new sense," he called it then— and later, at New Haven, he had distinguished its marks. It was a subject, he explained in the preface to his treatise, "on which my mind has been peculiarly intent, ever since I first entered on the study of divinity," and, he might have added, on which he speculated in his early miscellanies. Now, preparation done, he turns his mind fully to it, narrowing even further his concerns. "[M]y design is somewhat diverse from the design of what I have formerly published, which was to show the distinguishing marks of a work of the Spirit of God, in-

cluding both his common, and saving operations; but what I aim at
now, is to show the nature and signs of the gracious operations of God's
Spirit, by which they are to be distinguished from all things whatsoever that the minds of men are the subjects of, which are not of a saving
nature." And now, the fires of the revival banked, he leaves off history
and anecdotes and composes instead a treatise, his first, more like the
strict inquiries of his Stockbridge exile than the faithful narratives of
his Northampton pastorate, though impassioned still and experiential.
About love, *Religious Affections* is couched in the language of love.

Part I borrows the form of its provenance, the sermon, and opens
on the nature and importance of the affections with an explication of
the text, "Whom having not seen, ye love: in whom, though now ye
see him not, yet believing, ye rejoice with joy unspeakable, and full of
glory" (1 Pet. 1:8). The doctrine concludes simply, "True religion, in
great part, consists in holy affections," the conditional phrase a caveat
against exclusivity and excess. The affections differ "nothing at all"
from the inclination or the will except in degree, being the "more
vigorous and sensible" exercise of that faculty, but, Edwards admits, a
"somewhat imperfect" language with "loose and unfixed" meanings
may still cause some confusion. The affections differ from the passions—passions are more sudden and violent in their effect upon animal spirits, the mind "less in its own command"—and are of two sorts,
approving and disapproving: love, hope, and joy arise from the first;
hate, fear, and anger, from the second; pity and zeal, from both. And
the affections differ from pallid promises of the well-intentioned. "That
religion which God requires, and will accept, does not consist in weak,
dull and lifeless wouldings,"—Edwards's coinage—"raising us but a
little above a state of indifference: God, in his Word, greatly insists
upon it, that we be in earnest, fervent in spirit, and our hearts vigor-
ously engaged in religion." The evidence from the Bible vouchsafes the
affections time and again as the "spring of men's actions," the source
of their conversion, the fulness of the saints, the "true gold" of heaven,
the example of Christ, the design of the ordinances, and, as love, the
"fountain" of all else. Without the affections, the heart hardens, for
sin, as Edwards defines it, "radically and fundamentally consists in
what is negative, or privative, having its root and foundation in a
privation or want of holiness." Thus it is "clearly and abundantly evident, that true religion lies very much in the affections" and that critics
of the revival erred in discarding them indiscriminately. The "right
way"—Edwards's logical, middle ground—would have been to accept

some of them, reject others, "separating between the wheat and the chaff, the gold and the dross, the precious and the vile." And with that problem met, preachers and people would know the affections, move them and be moved by them "sensibly and strongly."

Signs uncertain and certain. Edwards repeats the pattern and, indeed, much of the substance of the third section of *Some Thoughts* in Part II of his treatise on the affections as he picks his way through a thicket of twelve uncertain signs. "'Tis no sign that affections are right, or that they are wrong" if they are intense or "raised very high," if they have "great effects on the body," promote fluency, arise out of self or Scripture, have "an appearance of love in them," seem numberless, consume time or prayers, or instill confidence in the affected. As he had in *Faithful Narrative,* he questions "the steps of a particular established scheme" for conversion and does it with signal economy: "We are often in Scripture expressly directed to try ourselves by the *nature* of the fruits of the Spirit; but nowhere by the Spirit's *method* of producing them." Again, as he had a decade earlier, he questions whether anyone can judge a conversion other than his own. "The true saints have not such a spirit of discerning, that they can determine who are godly, and who are not. For though they know experimentally what true religion is, in the internal exercise of it; yet these are what they can neither feel, nor see in the heart of another."

From such restraints and ambivalence—to each uncertain sign there is an inevitable "on the other hand"—Edwards turns in Part III to the "distinguishing signs of the truly gracious and holy affections," again, twelve, but more scriptural now and detailed, four times longer, in fact, than Part II. Yet, however fixed and certain the signs seem to be, he warns against presumption, citing man's fallibility and God's sovereign will, and discounts the possibility that any set of rules, even his, could somehow penetrate the "high conceit" of the hypocrite. Set off by roman numerals—uncertainty is numbered in arabic—each sign follows the triadic form of the sermon, less the initial biblical text, and each is self-contained, referring for the most part to no sign but itself. Together the twelve signs test the holy affections of true religion and constitute for Edwards the saving operation of the Spirit of God.

"Affections that are truly spiritual and gracious do arise from those influences and operations on the heart, which are *spiritual, supernatural* and *divine*," Edwards begins, explicating each of the critical terms, citing Scripture and annotating at length, often from Thomas Shepard and Solomon Stoddard, his grandfather. The Spirit of God infuses a

"new sense" in spiritual man, "what some metaphysicians call a new
simple idea," what Edwards, borrowing from an unacknowledged John
Locke, does as well. Natural man can neither know nor imagine this
new, divine principle, "no more than a man without a sense of tasting
can conceive of the sweet taste of honey"—an echo of *A Divine and
Supernatural Light* a dozen years earlier—nor the deaf "the melody of a
tune," nor the blind "the beauty of a rainbow." And because this
"lightsome" sense is founded upon "new principles of nature," it radically alters man, the whole of him, profoundly affecting all his faculties but creating none. The seal or earnest of the Spirit is a "vital,
gracious, sanctifying communication and influence," not the immediate revelation or "inward voice" of enthusiasts nor yet the delusive
shows of Satan, vain imaginings in ink upon paper or in "leaf-gold."

Gracious affections are grounded in the "transcendently excellent
and amiable nature of divine things, as they are in themselves," in
God's sovereignty and His *gloria,* not in "any conceived relation" to
the self or arising out of self-love, a condition of natural not spiritual
man. Affections are "primarily founded on the loveliness of the moral
excellency of divine things," as distinguished from natural excellency,
Edwards says of the third sign, much as moral good differs from natural. True saints perceive the beauty of God's holiness with "a new
supernatural sense," a sixth sense, as it were—"in its whole nature
diverse from any former kinds of sensations of the mind"—and it "cap-
tivates" and "delights" them.

Annihilation and the sign of signs.   The fourth sign describes
"the mind's being enlightened, rightly and spiritually to understand
and apprehend divine things," by the "sensations of a new spiritual
sense." Such understanding involves not merely the speculative faculty
of the mind but, more important, the active faculty of the heart and
will—what Edwards terms "sensible knowledge"—and differs markedly from natural understanding much as moral excellency differs from
natural. Thus the new sense, the key to holy affections, unlocks Edwards's epistemology as it had his aesthetics. The fifth sign describes
the conviction and certainty—and the immediacy both imply—that
arises out of the new sense perception, or, more directly out of the
"illumination" of the spiritual understanding and testifies to the truth
of the Bible and the beauty of God "there exhibited." The saint knows,
then, by intuition and by reason, "but it is without any long chain of
arguments; the argument is but one, and the evidence direct; the mind
ascends to the truth of the gospel but by one step, and that is its divine

glory." The sixth sign, humiliation, or man's conviction of his sinfulness, his "utter insufficiency, despicableness, and odiousness," attends the affections and, depending upon its source in natural things or spiritual, is either *"legal"* or *"evangelical."* For example, if a man were to renounce wealth and pleasure and "worldly inclinations" under threat of the law or by the tug of conscience, that would be legal self-denial; but if he were to renounce his "dignity and glory," empty himself, and "as it were renounce himself, and annihilate himself," and if he were to do that "freely and from his very heart," that would be self-denial of another sort and humility of an evangelical kind.

In the seventh sign, gracious affections are attended by "a change in nature," such that "the old man is put off and the new man put on." After the "first discoveries," there is a slow progress throughout life, a "continued conversion and renovation of nature," until the saint is "brought to perfection in glory." In the eighth, the affections "beget and promote" the temper of Christ, love and meekness, forgiveness and mercy, and fortitude—"strength of mind, through grace"—to check unruly passions and engage the "good affections." In the ninth, they "soften the heart" and make tender the spirit, eschew boldness and noise, and, following Christ, "turn a heart of stone more and more into a heart of flesh." In the tenth, like "God's workmanship," they reveal a "beautiful symmetry and proportion," a balance in saints of joy and comfort, on the one hand, and "godly sorrow and mourning for sin," on the other. Unlike people who are religious "by fits and starts," who, like comets, are "very unsteady and irregular," blaze for a moment and then disappear, true saints are like "the fixed stars, which, though they rise and set, are often clouded, yet are steadfast in their orb, and may truly be said to shine with a constant light." In the eleventh, they differ from other affections in this: kindling them is like kindling a flame, "the higher it is raised, the more ardent it is; and the more it burns, the more vehemently does it tend and seek to burn."

Gracious affections end in Christian practice, the twelfth sign, what Edwards calls the "work and business" of life, an account twice as long as any other, "the chief of all the signs of grace." Christian practice "implies" conformity, commitment, and persistence and is "much to be preferred to the method of the first convictions, enlightenings and comforts in conversion, or any immanent discoveries or exercises of grace whatsoever, that begin and end in contemplation." As the Bible "plainly teaches," it is the public and necessary proof of private conviction, the outward expression of an inward experience: "by their fruits ye shall know them" (Matt. 7:20), the most familiar among the many texts Edwards cites. Reason teaches much the same thing, that deeds are "more faithful interpreters" of the mind than words, and that free will, for example, is best understood by effects rather than means, by "the doing of it," an argument Edwards will make at considerable length almost a decade later. Thus Christian practice is the "best evidence" of sincerity and grace, the substance of Scripture and conscience, the "proper trial," the *principal sign.*" It is "grace made perfect," the "most proper" proof of repentance and salvation, of love and humility and fortitude, of gracious longings and holy joy.

It is also proper proof of a change in Edwards. Because the twelfth sign demands that the scheme of affections culminate in a public act, not in the privacy of the heart, it alters all that went before it. After the enthusiasm of a decade—and its collapse—and after his most expressive narrative of heart religion, the last and longest of the signs suggests more than a formal gesture of pastoral care, the kind of practical "use" that closes his many sermons. The mature reckoning of experience might better account for it; the need for order and moderation, perhaps; the tempering effect of hostile claims. Whatever the cause, the "sign of signs" of *Religious Affections* was surely a sign of the times. Another was Edwards's call for a concert of prayer less than two years later. By May 1749 the Reverend Joseph Bellamy would write to one of the authors of the preface to *Humble Attempt* that "not half the Country have ever So much as heard of Mr. Edwards peice [sic] upon the *Scotland Concert.*"[31] Such were the times.

On Barren Ground

Concert of prayer.   Published in early 1748, the 188-page book hints at its own desperation on the title page: *An Humble Attempt To promote Explicit Agreement And Visible Union of God's People in Extraordinary Prayer For the Revival of Religion and the Advancement of Christ's Kingdom on Earth, pursuant to Scripture-Promises and Prophecies concerning the last Time.*[32] The preface by five local ministers offers small comfort: "As to the author's ingenious observations on the prophecies, we entirely leave them to the reader's judgment." They have in mind his reading of the apocalyptic vision in the book of Revelation and the time of the slaying of the witnesses. Edwards held that the slaughter took place before the Reformation, not, as many chiliasts argued, immediately before the second coming, and so his call for a concert of prayer was not, he thought, a summons to willful death. "Upon the whole, I think there appears to be no reason from the prophecy concerning the two witnesses (Rev. 11), to expect any such general and terrible destruction of the church of Christ, before the utter downfall of Antichrist, as some have supposed; but good reason to determine the contrary." That aside, Edwards sanctions a world-wide union of prayer in order to recover the authority of evangelical Christianity abroad and, in a note of lamentation and prophecy, in his own Northampton. "How much is that kind of religion, that was professed and much experienced and practiced, in the first, and apparently the best times of New England, grown and growing out of credit? What fierce and violent contentions have been of late among ministers and people, about things of a religious nature? How much is the gospel ministry grown in contempt, and the work of the ministry, in many respects, laid under uncommon difficulties, and even in danger of sinking amongst us? How many of our congregations and churches rending in pieces?"

Humble Attempt is divided into three parts—a short history of the concert of prayer, the scriptural imperatives for it, and the practical and theoretical objections to it[33]—and begins like its sermonic source, with an explication of its text (Zech. 8:20–22) and a statement of its doctrine, "that it is a very suitable thing, and well-pleasing to God, for many people, in different parts of the world" to unite in common prayer, "which shall bring on" Christ's kingdom. Though the immediate occasion for the project was an initiative from several Scots ministers in a "Memorial lately sent over into America," Edwards had early learned the efficacy of public prayer. In "Personal Narrative" he recalls the boyhood tabernacle in the swamp that he shared with friends; in *Faithful Narrative* he tells of the prayer societies that in time led many of the young to surprising conversions; and in *Some Thoughts* he searches for "some contrivance" to unite "all God's people in America" in fasting and prayer "on the same day" to counter the "lukewarmness and unprofitableness" that followed the Great Awakening.[34] Now, five years later, he takes up the Scots cause and publicly defends it.

Edwards lists nine "motives to a compliance" with the proposed concert in the second part of *Humble Attempt*, citing text after biblical text, omitting many more "for brevity's sake." Thus "there is *yet remaining*" great work to be done, according to Scripture, to advance the kingdom of Christ, "an event unspeakably happy and glorious" for which He "prayed and labored and suffered," the *"main season"* of His success.

Not only does the "'whole creation'" await the day and the "whole Bible" encourage it, but current events and the changed times demand it: the "bloody war" in Canada, the "great decay" in New England, and the "great apostasy and provocation" the world over. And, to put it simply and somewhat differently, a union of prayer is "beautiful." "A civil union, or an harmonious agreement upon men in the management of their secular concerns, is amiable; but much more a pious union, and sweet agreement in the great business for which man was created, and had powers given him beyond the brutes; even the business of religion; the life and soul of which is love."

The third (and longest) part of *Humble Attempt* answers two series of objections to the proposal, the first, that it focusses too much on human invention, and the second, that its timing is unscriptural. The first series of three objections Edwards dismisses out of hand: a union of prayer binds no one, neither is it *"whimsical"* to join in extraordinary prayer *"at the same time"* nor yet Pharisaical: all manner of fast days and thanksgiving days are set and kept by agreement. His answer to the second series of three engages him more fully because it challenges his reading of key passages in Revelation—the prophecy of the sixth vial, for instance (Rev. 16:12–16)—and requires him to discredit Moses Lowman, the chief source of his renewed interest in the apocalypse, on his order of events and the precise timing of them: the Antichrist now reigns and will for another 270 years, Lowman claimed. "As to his particular scheme of seven periods, so divided and limited, and so obviously ranked in such order, and following one another in such direct and continued succession, and each ending in a state of peace, safety and happiness to the church of God, it seems to me to be more ingenious than solid, and that many things might be said to demonstrate it not to be founded in the truth of things, and the real design of the divine author of this prophecy." On the other hand, the waning influence of the pope in Catholic Europe and the "miraculous taking" of Cape Breton from the French in 1745 (and its supply of fish, "which makes no small part of the food and support of popish countries") assure Edwards that the prophecy of the sixth vial has already begun. And so he urges his readers to comply "calmly and deliberately" with the Scots proposal and hopes "that there may not be an end" to it, even after the allotted seven years of its life.

The death and life of a saint.   Edwards completed the manuscript for *Humble Attempt* in late summer 1747, probably a month or so after David Brainerd came to the King Street parsonage for the last time on 25 July; he died there on 9 October. Three days later Edwards delivered the funeral sermon, *True Saints,* based on 2 Cor. 5:8, "We are confident, I say, and willing rather to be absent from the body, and to be present with the Lord." To the customary praise for his "very considerable" learning, his "great insight into human nature," and his "extraordinary gifts for the pulpit," though Edwards admits he "never had the opportunity to hear him preach," the application includes references to Brainerd's diary (and lengthy passages from it in four notes) and Edwards's remembrance of his last words and hours.

But a few days before his death he desired us to sing a Psalm that was concerning the prosperity of Zion, which he signified that his mind was engaged in the thoughts of, and desires after, above all things; and at his desire we sang a part of the 102nd Psalm. And when we had done, though he was then so low that he could scarcely speak, he so exerted himself that he made a prayer very audibly, wherein besides praying for those present and for his own congregation, he earnestly prayed for the reviving and flourishing of religion in the world.[35]

Brainerd was "an example" to stir others, Edwards thought, and so he spent the better part of a year editing Brainerd's written account of his "inward exercises and experiences," another in a series of case histories that began with Abigail Hutchinson and Phebe Bartlet in *Faithful Narrative* and ended with Sarah Edwards in *Some Thoughts.*

Life of Brainerd (1749) has a three-part structure, though one less like the sermonic form Edwards habitually used than the editorial format the work required: preface, text, and afterword ("Reflections and Observations on the preceding Memoirs of Mr. Brainerd").[36] Though the first and last parts are clearly his own, the text reveals Edwards's hand as well. Apart from the marginalia he provided and his decision to reproduce only those parts of the journal not already in print, Edwards changed Brainerd's words and, more often, his thought by careful omission. Sometimes Edwards cuts unaccountably—"near a thick bunch of hazels"; other times he drops a telling metaphor—"I felt something like a criminal at the bar waiting for his sentence, excepting this, I felt but little concern which way my case went"—and with it sentence upon sentence of despair. He had called attention to Brainerd's "imperfection" in his preface—"he was one who by his constitution and natural temper was so prone to melancholy and dejection of spirit"—but Edwards believed Brainerd's "clear thought" and "exact

judgment" kept him from enthusiasm and "warm imagination" and
that he knew the difference between melancholy and "godly sorrow."
Edwards was somewhat less certain about his readers.

On reflection, he thought Brainerd and his wrestling with his soul
and the souls of the Indians of the Six Nations—case histories themselves—was proof of true religion and, in images of stars and streams,
an example of its constant and living ways.

His religion was not like a blazing meteor, or like a flaming comet (or a
"wandering star," as the apostle Jude calls it, verse 13) flying through the
firmament with a bright train; and then quickly going out in perfect darkness:
but more like the steady lights of heaven; that are constant principles of light,
though sometimes hid with clouds. Nor like a land flood which flows far and
wide with a rapid stream, bearing down all afore it, and then dried up; but
more like a stream fed by living springs, which though sometimes increased
by showers, and at other times diminished by drought, yet is a constant
stream.[37]

Life of Brainerd, Edwards observes, distinguishes true religion from
false and experimental piety from enthusiasm; it confirms the doctrine
of grace and confounds the Arminians; it teaches the ministry, and
Christians in general, "the right way of practicing religion"; and it
"excite[s] and encourage[s] God's people to earnest prayers": in short,
it is a guide to right awakening and a gloss to Edwards's published
work of a decade. Finally, he claims that Brainerd's death and dying,
especially his visit to the Boston commissioners, was a "special and
remarkable" providence of God to remind New England of the spiritual
plight of the Indians. Another death, less than a year after Brainerd's,
only deepened his concern.

Qualifications for dismissal.   On 26 June 1748, Edwards delivered the funeral sermon for his uncle John Stoddard, who had "a far
greater knowledge than any other person in the land, of the several
nations of Indians in these northern parts of America, their tempers,
manners, and the proper way of treating them" and who, in 1734 and
in Edwards's presence, had proposed the Stockbridge mission. But *A
Strong Rod* (Ezek. 19:12) was more than a reminder to Edwards of the
plight of the Six Nations nearby. Stoddard had been chief justice of the
Court of Common Pleas in Hampshire County, judge of probate, and
chief colonel of the regiment, a public man of authority, "*a great man,*"
and, in words touched perhaps with more than sorrow, "probably one

of the ablest politicians that ever New England bred." Most important, Stoddard had been a close supporter—in the bad-book episode, for instance—and a friend to his beliefs. He was, Edwards reports, "a wise casuist, as I know by the great help I have found from time to time by his judgment and advice in cases of conscience, wherein I have consulted him."[38] Now, as Edwards prepared to overturn forty years of Northampton's communion practice, half of them of his administering, he could use the authority of one Stoddard to challenge the authority of another. Without it, he suspected, he could very well lose his own.

The first sentence of his preface to *Humble Inquiry* (1749) acknowledges the difficulty. "My appearing in this public manner on that side of the question, which is defended in the following sheets, will probably be surprising to many, as it is well known, that Mr. Stoddard, so great and eminent a divine, and my venerable predecessor in the pastoral office over the church in Northampton, as well as my own grandfather, publicly and strenuously appeared in opposition to the doctrine here maintained." Later in the preface, tracing his path of change, Edwards recalls that he "imbibed from his [grandfather's] books, even from my childhood"—he quotes often from them in the pages following—and "conformed" to his practice, though not without misgivings. Still, he deferred to his grandfather's "authority" until, with more experience and study, he could examine the practice "more impartially," in time rejecting it, even at the risk of "my own reputation, future usefulness, and my very subsistence." Within a year he lost all three, even though his small quarto volume of 136 pages went largely unread.[39]

Divided into three parts—the question stated, eleven propositions examined, twenty objections answered[40]—*Humble Inquiry* is an exacting scriptural defense of earlier Puritan practice, not so much in the wealth of its citations as in the niceness of its argument, at times, "an easy mathematical demonstration." For Edwards in the spring of 1749, admission to full church membership was a matter no less exact. Only those who were "in profession" and judged "godly and gracious" by others ought to be admitted to the communion and the privileges of the visible church. The communion was not, as Stoddard taught and Northampton learned, a converting ordinance open to all but the scandalous; it was, rather, the seal of the covenant open to the saint and visible to other saints. "Real saints or converts are those that are in the eye of God; visible saints or converts are those who are so in the eye of

man; not his bodily eye, for thus no man is a saint any more in the eye
of a man than he is in the eye of a beast; but the eye of his mind, which
is his judgment or esteem." To visibility Edwards adds the need to
"verbally" own the covenant in a "public act" as an expression of the
"consent of the heart," much like the marriage covenant. The church,
then, is visible and professing, separated from the mass of the unconverted and "united by the bond of *Christian brotherly love*," as the par-
ables of Jesus and the writings of the apostles make "abundantly
manifest." In much the same way, the Lord's Supper is a joining together—a communion—of two parties in a "mutual solemn profession"
of the covenant of grace, Christ's minister and a visible saint openly
professing through signs. "The established signs in the Lord's supper
are fully equivalent to words; they are a renewing and reiterating the
same thing which was done *before*; only with this difference, that now
it is done by *speaking signs,* whereas before it was by *speaking sounds.*"

The rest of *Humble Inquiry,* more than a third of the text, anticipates
objections and answers twenty of them by the same hermeneutics and
logic that created them. Here, for example, Edwards begins to answer
the second objection to his scheme, that he equates visible saints with
God's people, often an impious lot in the Old Testament.

The argument proves too much, and therefore nothing at all. . . . For those
Jews which it is alleged were called God's people, and yet were so notoriously,
openly, and obstinately wicked, had neither any visibility of true piety, nor
yet of that moral sincerity in the profession and duties of the true religion,
which the opponents themselves suppose to be requisite in order to a proper
visible holiness, and a due admission to the privileges and ordinances of the
church of God. None will pretend that these obstinate idolaters and impious
wretches had those qualifications which are now requisite in order to an admission to the Christian sacraments. And therefore to what purpose can they
bring this objection?[41]

Other objections measure the new dispensation by the old—"perhaps
no part of divinity [is] attended with so much intricacy"—and baptism
by profession, the called by the chosen, the "tendency" of communion
by its "divine appointment," saints by hypocrites, grandson by grandfather. Edwards dismisses charges of inconvenience—"Some have found
great fault even with the *creation* of the world, as being very inconve-
niently done"—and impossibility: it is a "glaring absurdity" for saint
and sinner to meet at the Lord's table. And so he concludes *Humble*

Inquiry much as he began it, on a personal note. "I am sensible, it will be very difficult for many to be truly impartial to this affair; their prejudices being very great against the doctrine which I have maintained." All he asks is a fair reading and a reasonable reply, one free of both "dogmatical assertion and passionate reflection," and, if in print, that the author "set his name to his performance."

Two years later Solomon Williams, a kinsman, did set his name to *The True State of the Question Concerning the Qualifications Necessary to Lawful Communion in the Christian Sacraments* (1751), a page-by-page refutation. A year after that, 1752, Edwards replied with *Misrepresentations Corrected, And Truth vindicated,* but by then the issue was moot. The title page said as much: "By Jonathan Edwards, M.A., Minister of the Gospel at Stockbridge."

Chapter Five
Careful and Strict Inquiries

At the close of his ordination sermon for Job Strong on 28 June 1749, Jonathan Edwards explains the candor of his remarks by the sense he had of the end of things. "If you think I have spoken something freely to you, I hope it will be considered, that this is probably the last time you will ever hear me speak from the pulpit, and that I shall never see you again till we see one another in the invisible eternal world, where these things will open to us all in their just importance."[1] A year later, Edwards closes another farewell sermon, this one to his Northampton congregation of more than twenty-three years, in much the same way, breaking through the bitterness palpable on that first sabbath in July. "And let us remember, and never forget our future solemn meeting on that great day of the Lord, that day of infallible decision, and of the everlasting and unalterable sentence."[2] A month later, 4 August, he writes of his "small acquaintance" with revivals and the "stupidity" and "profane and atheistical spirit" that often follow an awakening. "Counterfeits of grace," he calls them, in the eight-page preface to *True Religion Delineated,* by the Reverend Joseph Bellamy,[3] like Samuel Hopkins, a Yale graduate (class of 1735) and a one-time student at the King Street parsonage.

Later that month he preaches from his pulpit—he would do that a dozen times more in the summer and fall following his dismissal—on "The Peace which Christ gives his true Followers." The text from John 14:27 begins, "Peace I leave with you, my peace I give unto you." The context, the opening lines of the sermon, must have seemed to many who heard it an unnecessary exegesis: "These words are part of a most affectionate and affecting discourse that Christ had with his disciples the same evening in which he was betrayed, knowing that he was to be crucified the next day." The doctrine of the sermon distinguishes between the legacy of Christ to true saints and "those things which the men of this world bequeath to their children," the river merchants of the Valley, perhaps, and their last wills of "stately mansions, and vast treasures of silver, gold, jewels, and precious things, fetched from both the Indies, and from every side of the globe of the earth."[4]

Points in Dispute, Part One: The Will

From Sabbath to Sabbath. By mid-November, as he wrote a friend, Northampton had heard enough. "The committee, that have the care of supplying the pulpit have asked me to preach, the greater part of the time since my dismission, when I have been at home; but it has seemed to be with much reluctance that they have come to me, and only because they could not get the pulpit supplied otherwise; and they have asked me only from Sabbath to Sabbath. In the mean time, they have taken much pains, to get somebody else to preach to them." Failing that, his biographer recalls, the committee voted that it was "not agreeable to their minds" to have him preach to them at all; "they carried on public worship among themselves, and without any preaching, rather than to invite Mr. Edwards!"[5] In December, he received an invitation to become minister to the Indian mission on the Housatonic, not far from the New York border, and in early August he was installed there. On 16 October 1751, sixteen months after his dismissal, family and household goods followed him out of Northampton the fifty miles to Stockbridge and a new life.

For nearly seven years Edwards managed the affairs of the mission, winning out over the rival Williamses, and lectured from old sermon notes. Occasionally, he left the settlement. Before the Synod of New York, gathered in Newark, New Jersey, on 28 September 1752, he preached *True Grace* (James 2:19), a sermon that harks back to *A Divine and Supernatural Light* and the signs of grace he first drew nearly twenty years before. "[I]t may be inferred, by parity of reason, that nothing that damned men do, or ever will experience, can be any sure sign of grace"—not speculative knowledge, belief of truth, "awakenings and terrors of conscience," convictions of guilt, longings after Christ, or visions of heaven. Saving grace, unlike common grace, is "a divine light in the souls of saints" that glorifies God and gives them a "sense of the supreme holy beauty and comeliness of divine things." Such grace, Edwards tells the assembled ministers in Newark, is the "daystar risen in the heart."[6] For the most part, though, he stayed in Stockbridge, tended to pastoral cares, married off three daughters, kept up with his correspondence, and wrote at some length about free will and original sin and, more briefly, about true virtue and the end of the world.

An Arminian obsession. The central issue of Edwards's orthodox theology—"I should not take it at all amiss, to be called a Calvinist," he wrote in 1753—and of his Arminian opposition was the problem of free will or, in the terms he intended to solve it, the doctrine of necessity. "The subject is of such importance," he claimed, "as to *demand* attention, and the most thorough consideration."[7] It certainly had demanded his. In early 1741, he reported to Bellamy that he had been engaged "pretty thoroughly in the study of the Arminian Controversy" and had written "considerably upon it in my private Papers," but he needed "the best Book on the Arminian side" on free will, because "I don't Know but I shall publish something after a while on that Subject." Six years later, in the summer of 1747, the summer of David Brainerd's fatal illness, he wrote the first of seven letters to the Rev. Dr. John Erskine, of Edinburgh, about the projected work and, as time went on, the frustrating delays. "I have thought of writing something particularly and largely on the Arminian controversy, in distinct discourses on the various points in dispute, to be published successively, beginning first with a discourse concerning Freedom of Will, and Moral Agency." A year later, on 31 August, he tells Erskine that he has been "diverted" from it by the preparation of the Brainerd diaries; on 14 October he adds that the *Life of Brainerd* has "remarkably hindered" him and that it will be "a considerable time" before he will have anything "ready for the press." Three days after his farewell sermon, he writes of the "troubles" that put an end to his studies: "I had made considerable preparation, and was deeply engaged in the prosecution of this design, before I was rent off from it by these difficulties, and if ever God should give me opportunity, I would again resume that affair." Two years later, on 7 July 1752, he writes Erskine from Stockbridge that he hopes to take up the Arminian controversy "in a short time," but by 23 November he reports that what began in August was "soon broken off." Less than five months later, on 14 April 1753, his first words to Erskine declare, "After many hindrances, delays and interruptions, Divine Providence has so favoured me, and smiled on my design of writing on the Arminian controversy, that I have almost finished the first draught."[8] The 294-page book was published early the following year as *A careful and strict Enquiry Into The modern prevailing Notions Of That Freedom of Will, Which is supposed to be essential To Moral*

Agency, Vertue and Vice, Reward and Punishment, Praise and Blame.[9]

Three years later the subject still demanded his attention and thorough consideration. In a letter, dated 25 July 1757, that would become appended to the third edition of the text, Edwards writes Erskine of the "vast importance" of the study to the "most important articles" of Christianity and that without it, "it is, to me, beyond doubt, that the friends of those great gospel truths, will but poorly maintain their controversy with the adversaries of those truths: they will be obliged often to dodge, shuffle, hide, and turn their backs; and the latter will have a strong fort, from whence they never can be driven, and weapons to use, which those whom they oppose will find no shield to screen themselves from; and they will always puzzle, confound, and keep under the friends of sound doctrine; and glory, and vaunt themselves in their advantage over them; and carry their affairs with an high hand, as they have done already for a long time past." A week later, on 3 August, Edwards again stresses the importance of the question of will and the "inconceivably pernicious" doctrine of self-determination, and he asks Erskine's forbearance. "Excuse me, sir, for troubling you with so much on this head. I speak from the fullness of my heart."[10] Within the year Edwards was dead. *Freedom of the Will*, it turned out, was the last of his works he would see in print.

The idea of order at Tierra del Fuego. Even by eighteenth-century practices of full disclosure, Edwards's title page tells much about his five-part inquiry: first, careful definitions of terms like *freedom, will,* and *contingency*; then, modern, that is, Arminian, notions of free will; next, essential connections between free will and moral agency and responsibility; after that, numbered errors in the Arminian contention; and finally, the fifth and shortest part, the doctrine of necessity and the five points of strict Calvinism.[11] The biblical text for the whole comes from Rom. 9:16, "It is not of him that willeth," and may, in its brevity, suggest the less than metaphysical turn of mind of *Freedom of the Will.* Scriptural citations, while still abundant, are concerned with only three questions of will—the evidences of God's foreknowledge, the acts of Jesus, and the authorship of sin—and are confined to a half dozen of the nearly forty sections that divide the argument. For the rest, Edwards confronts three theological antagonists—Thomas Chubb, Daniel Whitby, and Isaac Watts; a deist, an Anglican, and a Dissenter—and his philosophical mentor, John Locke. Though he usually keeps a proper distance from them, once in a while he closes in, with delight and devastating effect, as in this attack on the "utterly unintelligible and inconsistent" definition of an act by Chubb and others: "that it should be necessary, and not necessary; that it should be from a cause, and no cause; that it should be the fruit of choice and design, and not the fruit of choice and design; that it should be the beginning of motion or exertion, and yet consequent on previous exertion; that it should be before it is" and so on.

If some learned philosopher, who had been abroad, in giving an account of the curious observations he had made in his travels, should say, he "had been in Tierra del Fuego, and there had seen an animal which he calls by a certain name, that begat and brought forth itself, and yet had a sire and a dam distinct from itself; that it had an appetite, and was hungry before it had being; that his master, who led him, and governed him at his pleasure, was always governed by him, and driven by him as he pleased; that when he moved, he always took a step before the first step; that he went with his head first, and yet always went tail foremost; and this, though he had neither head nor tail": it would be no impudence at all, to tell such a traveler, though a learned man, that he himself had no notion or idea of such an animal as he gave an account of, and never had, nor ever would have.[12]

Common speech and terms of art. For all that, Edwards, not unlike Chubb and the others, lays the "foundation of his scheme" upon a series of careful definitions based upon "common speech" or "the ordinary use of language," and he begins Part I of his argument with a definition of the will. "And therefore I observe that the will (without any metaphysical refining) is plainly, that by which the mind chooses anything." Call it choosing, approving, liking, preferring, or desiring—Edwards quarrels with Locke over the last two—the will acts voluntarily in a present moment, so that "in every act of the will there is an act of choice" or "prevailing inclination" at that instant. Or, in an important formulation, "a man's doing as he wills, and doing as he pleases, are the same thing in common speech." What determines the will—Edwards calls it "that grand inquiry" in the second section—is the strongest motive immediately appearing to the mind as good, "the greatest apparent good." The will is invariably drawn to what is agreeable to the mind, to what "*suits*" or pleases it as an immediate and direct object of volition. "There is scarcely a plainer and more universal dictate of the sense and experience of mankind, than that, when men act voluntarily, and do what they please, then they do what suits them best, or what is most agreeable to them."

Yet not all words are so plainly understood nor their definitions so usual. Words like *necessary, impossible, unable,* and *contingent* are so connected to will or desire by habits of thought from childhood on that unless they are used "as terms of art," that is, in another sense entirely, they can only "deceive and confound." In a special, philosophical sense, *necessity* is "nothing different from certainty," or, to put it grammatically, "nothing else than the full and fixed connection between the things signified by the subject and predicate of a proposition, which affirms something to be true." There is nothing relative about necessity, nothing that implies or supposes opposition; it simply speaks to the "infallible connection" between things—in themselves, in the past, or in consequence—and to the existence of things. It is in this restricted sense that Edwards will try to prove the primary hypothesis of his argument, that "necessity is not inconsistent with liberty."

Edwards next distinguishes moral from natural necessity and inability much as he had distinguished moral from natural excellency in the third sign of *Religious Affections.* Moral necessity arises from moral causes, motives, or volitions: "the habits and dispositions of the heart"; natural necessity arises from natural causes, physical sensations, or demonstrated truths: gravity, pain, or sums in arithmetic. Natural inability differs from moral inability in this: in the first, nature prevents us from doing something even if we will—even a determined man has a natural inability to fly; in the second, the will prevents us from acting contrary to its disposition—a chaste woman may have a moral inability "to prostitute herself to her slave." Still, we err when we assume that a wicked man, for example, has a moral inability to love God if all he lacks is the will, because, strictly speaking, "a man can't be truly said to be unable to do a thing, when he can do it if he will." Reduced even further, "the very willing is in the doing."

In the last, the fifth section of Part I, Edwards considers freedom and agency as functional complements. A person may have freedom but his will cannot because "the will itself is not an agent that has a will." Freedom of the will is the power one has to choose and, in choosing, act. "Let the person come by his volition or choice how he will, yet, if he is able, and there is nothing in the way to hinder his pursuing and executing his will, the man is fully and perfectly free, according to the primary and common notion of freedom." And because a person acts freely and morally, he merits praise and reward, deserves blame and punishment, is, in short, responsible for his actions.

For Edwards, then, the question that beset his generation was misplaced: the point was not free will but free men, a matter of who, not what. Other thinkers, even contending ones like Thomas Hobbes and John Locke, agreed that if a man does as he pleases, he is free. "I think it impossible for anyone to rise higher in his conception of liberty than this," he wrote Erskine; "if any imagine they desire higher, and that they conceive of a higher and greater liberty than this, they are deceived, and delude themselves with confused ambiguous words, instead of ideas."[13] As he had insisted all along, it was a matter of "confused unmeaning words" and spasms of unreason, knots of language and logic that will and determination—his will and his determination—might untangle.

Argument from cause. The problem, as Edwards saw it in Part II, was not only that Arminians confuse action and agent, but that, given the proposition that the will determines itself, they were led willy-nilly to absurdity.

If the will determines the will, then choice orders and determines the choice: and acts of choice are subject to the decision, and follow the conduct of other acts of choice. And therefore if the will determines all its own free acts, then every free act of choice is determined by a preceding act of choice, choosing that act. And if that preceding act of the will or choice be also a free act, then by these principles, in this act too, the will is self-determined; that is, this, in like manner, is an act that the soul voluntarily chooses; or which is the same thing, it is an act determined still by a preceding act of the will, choosing that. And the like may again be observed of the last mentioned act. Which brings us directly to a contradiction: for it supposes an act of the will preceding the first act in the whole train, directing and determining the rest; or a free act of the will, before the first free act of the will. Or else we must come at last to an act of the will, determining the consequent acts, wherein the will is not self-determined, and so is not a free act, in this notion of freedom: but if the first act in the train, determining and fixing the rest, be not free, none of them all can be free; as is manifest at first view, but shall be demonstrated presently.[14]

Aside from such examples of close reasoning and Arminian evasions—some, Edwards has to admit, of "my own inventing"—he pauses in his pursuit to explain the rule and method of the whole free will enterprise: the argument from cause.

As he scrupulously defines it in section three, *cause* is "any antecedent, either natural or moral, positive or negative, on which an event, either a thing or the manner and circumstance of a thing, so depends, that it is the ground and reason, either in whole or in part, why it is, rather than not." Thus, he asserts, "nothing ever comes to pass without a cause," and thus, by inference, "what is self-existent must be from eternity, and must be unchangeable." For Edwards, the argument from cause is a divine given, "the first dictate of the common and natural sense which God hath implanted in the minds of all mankind, and the main foundation of all our reasonings about the existence of things, past, present, or to come." Without this "grand principle," we could not prove the existence of God (He is by His works), nor know the past (it is by its effects), nor explain an act of the will. It is as "repugnant to reason" to suppose that an act of the will is without cause as to suppose that the universe is. So for the rest of Part II, Edwards uses the argument from cause—and in section 11 on God's foreknowledge, the argument from Scripture—to unravel the Arminian notion, strand by absurd strand: indifferent volition, and contingency independent of necessity; passive motivation, and understanding independent of will. And so he concludes that "the will don't determine itself in any one of its own acts." Every act of the will must have a cause and every cause a cause just prior to it in an infinite regress, so that from first to last, cause and act stretch back without interruption to the beginning of being. As Edwards puts it, "every act of choice and refusal, depends on, and is necessarily connected with some antecedent cause; which cause is not the will itself, nor any act of its own, nor anything pertaining to the faculty, but something belonging to another faculty, whose acts go before the will, in all its acts, and govern and determine them every one." What governs and determines—and knows—the first act, of course, is God.

Responsibility by necessity. God is also the first example drawn in Part III—"the supreme moral Agent," Edwards calls Him—to explain how the Arminian notions of liberty and necessity deny agency and responsibility, the altogether human questions of virtue and vice, praise and blame, reward and punishment. To all His people, God is the fountain and perfect pattern of holiness and virtue, deserving infinite love and honor and praise; to the Arminians, or at least to the Dr. Whitby whom Edwards quotes, virtue in God is "'an empty name'" and deserves no praise because God is under necessity and "can't avoid being holy and good as he is; therefore no thanks to him for it." As usual, Edwards picks the argument apart by definition and logic, refraining from "endless" and "altogether needless" biblical texts to confute it. Yet in the following section he cites text after text to prove that the necessarily holy, human Christ deserves both praise and reward. "I have been the longer in the proof of this matter," he notes after several pages, "because I look upon it as a point clearly and absolutely determining the controversy between Calvinists and Arminians," that is, the place of necessity in moral responsibility. If Christ, the perfect pattern of obedience, deserves praise, then man in disobedience deserves blame, the Arminian notion of necessity notwithstanding. If man's imperfections are necessarily without blame, then why did Christ suffer and die and, in dying, purchase man's salvation? "What need therefore of Christ's dying, to satisfy for them?" Edwards asks, as he had twenty years earlier in "Justification by Faith Alone." "What need of his suffering, to satisfy for that which is no fault, and in its nature deserves no suffering? What need of Christ's dying, to purchase, that our *imperfect* obedience should be accepted, when according to their [the Arminians'] scheme, it would be unjust in itself, that any other obedience than *imperfect* should be required?"

Just as obedience does not relieve us of moral responsibility, so command does not. The answer lies in the *"original and determining"* inclination to act, for to act contrary to our disposition would mean that we can determine the first act of the will, and that, as Edwards has been at some pains to point out, is absurd. "['T]is true, the will, in every instance, acts by moral necessity, and is morally unable to act otherwise." Therefore, moral inability can no more excuse disobedience to a command than can sincerity or indifference, as the Arminians propose. In his moral arithmetic, Edwards tallies only the good we do and likens sincerity to "subtracting a thousand noughts from before a real number, which leaves the sum just as it was." The good we do, he continues, arises out of necessity from a virtuous or "friendly" heart, not an indifferent (and cold) one, as some claim. Indifference subverts choice by equating possibilities and by ignoring the habits of the heart. If no disposition of the heart (or inclination of the will) determines choice, then nothing in us can make us better or worse. One rock is no more vicious than another "because rattlesnakes have happened oftener to crawl over it." And if, as Edwards reports in the last section, motives and inducements count for little in the Arminian analysis, "Where then," he asks, "shall we find room for virtue and vice?" The opening section of Part IV locates it in the nature of both.

The limits and misuse of language.   Ironically, Edwards argues from cause to disprove cause. Virtue and vice are what they are by their nature, not by their cause: it is the nature of an act, not its origin, that deserves praise or blame, reward or punishment. "To say," as the Arminians do, "that vice don't consist in the thing which is vicious, but in its cause, is the same as to say, that vice don't consist in vice," a contradiction. Vice is an inclination or disposition of the will to choose evil, and choice, all would agree, entails responsibility. "'Tis a certain beauty or deformity that are *inherent* in that good or evil will, which is the *soul* of virtue and vice (and not in the *occasion* of it) which is their worthiness of esteem or disesteem, praise or dispraise, according to the common sense of mankind."

The remaining twelve sections of the last part of the *Inquiry* divide into problems of language and logic and observations on divine necessity, the whole yet another appeal to common sense and, like the argument in the first part, to common speech. The Arminians, Edwards writes, build the "mighty edifice" of their moral philosophy on the "sands, or rather on a shadow" of uncommon meanings. Their definition of action is "abstruse, inconsistent, and entirely diverse from the original sense of the word in common speech"; their notion of natural and moral necessity is "exceeding diverse" from that "commonly used" by both sides to the controversy; their failure to reconcile praise and blame with necessity lies in the "impropriety and ambiguity of terms" they use, terms "the common people" know by "*experience* and a *natural sensation*" of the rightness of a thing, not by some metaphysical quibble. To the Arminian charge that necessity makes machines of us, Edwards answers with a single-sentence paragraph that serves as well as any to summarize his argument on free will.

As to that objection against the doctrine which I have endeavored to prove, that it makes men no more than mere machines; I would say, that notwithstanding this doctrine, man is entirely, perfectly and unspeakably different from a mere machine, in that he has reason and understanding, and has a faculty of will, and so is capable of volition and choice; and in that, his will is guided by the dictates or views of his understanding; and in that his external actions and behaviors, and in many respect also his thoughts, and the exercises of his mind, are subject to his will; so that he has liberty to act according to his choice, and do what he pleases; and by means of these things, is capable of moral habits and moral acts, such inclinations and actions as according to the common sense of mankind, are worthy of praise, esteem, love and reward; or on the contrary, of disesteem, detestation, indignation and punishment.[15]

And to their charge that his doctrine of necessity differs little from the fatalism of the Stoics or the necessity of Thomas Hobbes, Edwards answers that Stoicism "came nearest to Christianity" of all ancient philosophies and that truth is not "spoiled" when shouted by the devil or penned by an English skeptic. Besides, he adds, "I must confess, it happens I never read Mr. Hobbes."

Edwards turns to language once again as he opens his observations on divine necessity, but it is not misuse that troubles him so much as the inability of language "to express precise truth." More especially, it is the inability of language to express "things in the mind of the incomprehensible Deity," things like "infinite *power*," "supreme *authority*," underived and independent "*will*" and "*wisdom*," things that belong to "*absolute sovereignty*." So described, God must act by necessity, for to act otherwise would be inconsistent with His excellent and perfect nature; that He acts by necessity according to His nature, and not by contingence, makes evil impossible to Him. "To suppose the divine will liable to be carried hither and thither at random, by the uncertain wind of blind contingence, which is guided by no wisdom, no motive, no intelligent dictate whatsoever (if any such thing were possible), would certainly argue a great degree of imperfection and meanness, infinitely unworthy of the deity." As well, necessity makes divine indifference impossible and renders another, perhaps more crucial, Arminian allegation an impertinence, that God is the author of sin. There is a "great difference," Edwards insists, between permitting sin and producing it; between being the "*orderer* of its certain existence" and being the "*actor* or *author* of it." To use a metaphor—in a work all but empty of them—there is a "vast difference between the sun's being the cause of the lightsomeness and warmth of the atmosphere, and brightness of gold and diamonds, by its presence and positive influence; and its being the occasion of darkness and frost, in the night, by its motion, whereby it descends below the horizon." If God is sinful, then the sun "must needs be black." No; the infinitely good God hates sin infinitely—"his will is really crossed in it"—and endures it in an infinite misery of pain and grief: He is not the maker of it, man is.

Calvinism triumphant.   Edwards presses the last encounters between Calvinist and Arminian into four, short closing sections. Arminian self-determination, he argues, can no more describe God's moral character than it can describe man's; it can no more solve the difficulty of when sin came into the world than it can solve the difficulty of whence it came. The Calvinist doctrine of necessity, on the other hand, explains each of these matters reasonably and is "the only medium" that proves the being of God. Not the "pernicious effects" of necessity but the "happy remedy" of liberty and contingence spreads licentiousness and atheism abroad. Finally, to scoff at the doctrine of necessity as so much fussy metaphysics is like saying an idea is weak because it is in a foreign tongue. "The question is not, whether what is said be metaphysics, physics, logic, or mathematics, Latin, French, English, or Mohawk? but, whether the reasoning be good, and the arguments truly conclusive?" There is nothing metaphysical or abstruse about the argument from cause, no "nice scholastic distinctions" about it. Arminians, not Calvinists, wrap themselves in verbal ambiguity, use words as "terms of art"—a phrase Edwards had earlier claimed for himself—and "improve" upon them metaphysically, "contrary to common sense, in a high degree," contrary even "to their own sense, which governs them in common life."

Thus the argument of the *Inquiry* ends. The brief conclusion, a separate part, indicates how the "grand article" of necessity confirms the five points of Calvinism—innate depravity, irresistible grace, absolute election, limited atonement, and the perseverance of the saints—and confounds the Arminian notion of liberty. For the rest, Edwards leaves to the "fair and impartial reader" to consider the argument and to the Bible (1 Cor. 1:20) to judge it: "Hath not God made foolish the wisdom of the world?"

A Great Christian Doctrine

Sin, by definition.   Once he resolved the question of the will, Edwards could turn to other "points in dispute" with the Arminians, as he had promised Erskine he would, and in the closing pages of the *Inquiry* he hints at one of them. "But it would require room that can't be here allowed," he explains, "fully to consider all the difficulties which have been started, concerning the first entrance of sin into the world." Yet in the spring of 1755, nearly a year after the publication of the *Inquiry,* Edwards turned not to the first entrance of sin into the world but to two other points in dispute, the end for which God created the world and the nature of true virtue. By the following summer he put both aside in rough draft to devote his "leisure hours," as his biographer put it, to a treatise on original sin, completing it between 26 May 1757, the date of the preface, and early fall, when he was offered the presidency of Princeton. He never saw it in print.

The Great Christian Doctrine of Original Sin defended by "the late Reverend and Learned Jonathan Edwards," was published that spring. A text from Matthew—"They that be whole need not a physician, but they that are sick" (9:12)—and passages in Latin from the ancient rabbis and the poet Juvenal crowd the title page. Samuel Finley added a brief account of Edwards's life derived from the "public Prints," observing that his language had "a noble Negligence" about it. The text itself ran to nearly four hundred octavo pages.[16]

Most of them are given over to a page-by-page reply to the "objections and arguings" of Dr. John Taylor's *The Scripture-Doctrine of Original Sin, Proposed to Free and Candid Examination* (1738), a book Edwards had "borrowed and read" before getting a copy of his own from Erskine in the summer of 1748.[17] Fully half the text, two of four parts, gathers scriptural evidence against Taylor from both testaments, from the first three chapters of Genesis and the fifth chapter of Romans mainly, a daunting show. Edwards pledges to "study brevity" and to eschew "the nature of things"—the stuff of philosophical inquiries and "'Metaphysicks!'"—for what is "plainly demonstrated by what has been shewn to be *fact*." But to those who might complain about the length of a study devoted so single-mindedly to such a demonstration, he pleads the "*great importance*" of the doctrine of original sin to "the whole gospel or doctrine of salvation" and, more practically, the need to counter "almost *every* argument" of the "specious" Taylor. That his "antidote," as he called it in his preface, ultimately failed had more to do with the virulent strain of Arminianism then abroad than with his compounded effort. In 1758 alone, five pamphlets on original sin were published in New England.[18]

"All mankind," Edwards proclaims at the start of Part I, "do constantly in all ages, without fail in any one instance, run into that moral evil, which is in effect their own utter and eternal perdition, in a total privation of God's favor and suffering of his vengeance and wrath." Moral evil arises from original sin, which he defines as both the "*innate sinful depravity of the heart*" and, as commonly understood, the "*imputation* of Adam's first sin" to posterity, or man's continued liability in Adam and in his punishment. Thus man's natural propensity to sin is "an universal, constant, infallible event"; the proof of that rests in the familiar argument from cause. "The natural dictate of reason shews, that where there is an effect, there is a cause, and a cause sufficient for the effect; because, if it were not sufficient, it would not be effectual: and that therefore, where there is a stated prevalence of effect, there is a stated prevalence in the cause: a steady effect argues a steady cause." Only God's saving grace can interrupt that chain of events and alter man's fixed nature and tendency to sin. "Grace is a sovereign thing," Edwards reminds his readers, "exercised according to the good pleasure of God, bringing good out of evil; the effect of it belongs not to the nature of things themselves, that otherwise have an ill tendency, any more than the remedy belongs to the disease; but is something altogether independent on it, introduced to oppose the natural tendency, and reverse the course of things." That natural tendency, which men "carry with them wherever they go," results in "the infinite heinousness of sin," because, as Edwards had pointed out in the *Inquiry,* it violates an infinite obligation to an infinite God, and no amount of personal merit or virtue can right the "vast over-balance." How "absurd" to think a woman good, "because, although she committed adultery, and that with the slaves and scoundrels sometimes, yet she did not do this so often as she did the duties of a wife."

The languages of proof.   For the rest, the first part addresses some of the standard objections raised against the doctrine of original sin and some of the consequences flowing from it. But Edwards puts off until the end of the study extended answers to such questions as the authorship of sin, infant damnation, and imputation, preferring instead to challenge Taylor on other, less critical matters first. To Taylor's observation that "we are no judges of the viciousness of men's character," Edwards offers in evidence his frontier life: "I think, I have sufficient reason, from what I know and have heard of the American Indians, to judge, that there are not many good philosophers among them; though the thoughts of their hearts, and the ideas and knowledge they have in their minds, are things invisible." To Taylor's argument that not man's nature but his "*free will* is cause sufficient" for his corruption, Edwards asks, "How comes it to pass, that the free will of mankind has been determined to evil, in like manner before the flood, and after the flood; under the law, and under the gospel; among both Jews and Gentiles, under the Old Testament; and since that, among Christians, Jews, Mohametans; among Papists and Protestants; in those nations where civility, politeness, arts and learning most prevail, and among the Negroes and Hottentots in Africa, the Tartars in Asia, and Indians in America, towards both poles, and on every side of the globe; in greatest cities, and obscurest villages; in palaces, and in huts, wigwams and cells under ground?" And to Taylor's "evasion" that sinfulness follows upon bad example rather than corrupt nature, Edwards

cites the example of Jesus few adults follow and the example of children
who sin "as soon as capable of it." Death, particularly the death of
infants, proves to Edwards "that men come sinful into the world," and
he undertakes to bury Taylor with scriptural texts and verbal nicety.
"We may well understand 'innocent' as included in the word 'righteous,' according to the language usual in Scripture, in speaking of
such cases of judgment and punishment; as is plain in Gen. 20:4; Ex.
23:7; Deut. 25:1; II Sam. 4:11; II Chron. 6:23; and Prov. 18:5." He
completes the task in even graver detail in the next two parts of his
treatise.

Part II explicates critical texts chiefly in Genesis and Romans that
Taylor had cited and examined in his *Scripture-Doctrine,* the central doc-
ument for Edwards, and his *Key to Apostolic Writings* and *Paraphrase on
the Epistle to the Romans,* complementary works. Typically, Edwards
tears a page from one of them and worries it to absurdity, as in this on
Adam and the family of man:

Dr. Taylor (p. 19) says, "A curse is pronounced upon the ground, but no curse
upon the woman and the man." And in pp. 321, 322 he insists, that the
ground only was cursed, and not the man: just as though a curse could ter-
minate on lifeless, senseless earth! To understand this curse otherwise than as
terminating upon man, through the ground, would be as senseless as to suppose the meaning to be "The ground shall be punished, and shall be miserable
for thy sake." Our author interprets the curse on the ground, of its being
encumbered with noxious weeds: but would these weeds have been any curse
on the ground, if there had been no inhabitants, or if the inhabitants had been
of such a nature, that these weeds should not have been noxious, but useful
to 'em?[19]

Edwards clings to Taylor's every word, turning to the Hebrew of the
Old Testament or the Greek of the New when English won't do:
"where Jacob says [in Gen. 31:39], 'That which was torn from beasts,
anochi achattenah'—which Dr. Taylor is pleased to translate, 'I was the
sinner': but is properly rendered, 'I expiated it'; the verb 'in pihel'
properly signifying 'to expiate.'" He pores over Buxtorf's *Concordance,*
searching out the Hebrew *jashar* applied to moral agents: "(if I have
not mis-reckoned) about 110 times in Scripture; and about an 100 of
them, without all dispute, to signify virtue, or moral rectitude (though
Dr. Taylor is pleased to say, the word don't generally signify a moral
character)." He sets parallel columns to gloss three verses in Romans

(5:12–14) that he insists Taylor misreads, though he allows that "two or three expressions" in the text still remain in "obscurity." He translates three verses from Virgil's *Aeneid* (IV, 365–67) in an attempt to distinguish the sense of Dido's words from David's—trope from fact— and Taylor's from his own sense of "born in sin."

Yet again the problem comes down to the uses of language, though not to the difference between common use and metaphysical that he had remarked in the *Inquiry* so much as the difference between literal and figurative apparent, for example, in the Bible. Words like *death, heart, light,* "and many others" have both an external or physical sense (the heart as muscle) and an internal or spiritual one (the heart as the seat of the affections), a point Edwards drives home, lexicon in hand. "'Tis especially common in Hebrew, and I suppose, other Oriental languages, that the same word that signifies something external, does no less properly and usually signify something more spiritual. So the Hebrew words used for 'breath,' have such a double signification; 'Neshama' signifies both 'breath' and 'soul'; and the latter as commonly as the former: 'ruach' is used for 'breath' or 'wind,' but yet more commonly signifies. 'spirit.' 'Nephesh' is used for 'breath,' but yet more commonly signifies 'soul.'" Taylor, of course, fails such distinctions and, necessarily, the substantative issues arising from them: the question of original righteousness, the nature of the threat of death, the notion of a federal head, the significance of "the children of men," and so on.

Superior and inferior principles. Shorter than Part II by more than a hundred pages and much narrower in its concerns, Part III snares Taylor once more in "the language of Scripture," this time on the nature and application of redemption. Edwards insists upon the necessary connection between Adam's sin and Christ's redemption— the doctrine of the fortunate fall—and judges Taylor's understanding of the old man and the new "unreasonable, and contrary to the utmost degree of scriptural evidence," no less so his understanding of repentance and conversion, circumcision of the heart and baptism of the spirit. For Edwards it is "a truth of the utmost certainty, with respect to *every* man, born of the race of Adam, by ordinary generation, that *unless he be born again, he cannot see the kingdom of God.*" That underscored, he next answers objections to his argument in Part IV, putting aside one of them by reference, but taking up another two with some care and even more ingenuity.

To the familiar Arminian canard that innate depravity precludes free

will, Edwards offers his *Inquiry* to any reader "willing to give himself
the trouble of consulting" it; to prove the "gross *inconsistencies*" of Taylor
on the matter, he simply quotes him against himself. To the old blas-
phemy about the authorship of sin, the tainted God, Edwards offers
the *Inquiry* again—"I must refer the reader to what I have said of it in
my discourses on the *Freedom of the Will*"—but now he argues, as he
had not then, the dual nature of created man. God implanted "two
kinds of principles" in man when first He made him, an *"inferior"* and
a *"superior"* kind, which, even at the risk of confusion, Edwards terms
"natural" and "supernatural." Of these "concreated or connate" principles, the first has to do with self-love and the appetites derived from
it, "what the Scriptures sometimes call *flesh*"; the second has to do with
divine love and man's righteousness and holiness flowing from it,
"which are called in Scripture the *divine nature.*"

In the beginning, the superior principles held "the throne," reigning
over the inferior impulses in man. But when Adam sinned, broke the
covenant, and fell under the curse, "these superior principles left his
heart: for indeed God then left him; that communion with God, on
which these principles depended, entirely ceased; the Holy Spirit, that
divine inhabitant, forsook the house." Superior principles "immediately" and "wholly" ceased then, much as "light ceases in a room, when
the candle is withdrawn." Inferior principles became "absolute masters
of the heart," turned "all things upside down" and, like a raging fire,
possessed "the whole house." Thus, Edwards concludes, Adam's sin
was privative and negative—it arose form his own nature when God
withdrew His—and it was continuous. "For Adam's posterity are from
him and as it were in him, and belonging to him, according to an
established course of nature, as much as the branches of a tree are,
according to a course of nature, from the tree, in the tree, and belonging to the tree; or (to make use of the comparison which Dr. Taylor
himself chooses and makes use of from time to time, as proper to il-
lustrate the matter) 'just as the acorn is derived from the oak.'" Taylor's
cliché duly noted, Edwards spends an inventive two dozen pages on
the crucial questions of imputation and identity.

Identity and the theory of continued creation.   That God
treated the first man as the first of men implies that Adam and the
children of Adam constitute a *"oneness* or *"identity"* and that they share
his nature, his apostasy, and his guilt. That God created Adam and his
nature prior to his apostasy and his guilt implies that the same order
obtains in the children of Adam, that sharing his nature, they follow

the steps of his fall. "The first depravity of heart, and the imputation of that sin, are both the consequences of that established union [of Adam and his posterity]: but yet in such order, that the evil disposition is *first,* and the charge of guilty *consequent*; as it was in the case of Adam himself." Suppose, Edwards adds in a long footnote, that Adam and his posterity coexisted, united in "*one* complex person, or *one* moral whole" so that as the head (or the heart) acted the members of the body responded in the same order; where or when that took place would not "hinder things succeeding in the same order"; hence, everywhere and at all times, the disposition to sin precedes the imputation of it or, more personally, our guilt follows upon our nature. Still, if each of us though related to Adam is distinct from him, should God treat us as one in his apostasy? The answer to that lies in language—what we mean by *sameness* or *oneness*—and in the laws of nature.

A great tree is "one plant with the little sprout" it grew from, bigger now, distinct, "perhaps not one atom the very same: yet God, according to an established law of nature, has in a constant succession communicated to it many of the same qualities, and most important properties, as if it were one." Infant to sage, the same law of nature applies, slightly amended. Personal identity is essentially—Locke, Edwards reports, had said "wholly"—"*same consciousness*" continued in time; it "depends wholly on a law of nature; and so, on the sovereign will and agency of God." But God not only creates being, He preserves and upholds it in time, immediately and continually, moment by successive moment, because "what is *past* entirely ceases, when *present* existence begins." And so "God's *preserving* created things in being is perfectly equivalent to a *continued creation,* or to his creating those things out of nothing at *each moment* of their existence." The first creation differs from the last "only *circumstantially,*" and the first apostasy from the last not at all. What exists now is a "*new effect*": though like the past, it is not the same with the past. "All dependent existence whatsoever is in a constant flux, ever passing and returning; renewed every moment, as the colors of bodies are every moment renewed by the light that shines upon them; and all is constantly proceeding from God, as light from the sun." Only God's "*arbitrary constitution,*" the divine will and wisdom, unites the moments of color or existence in identity or oneness; only as He "*treats them as one*" are they one, a man no less than a tree, mankind no less than a man. "And I am persuaded," Edwards concludes, "no solid reason can be given, why God, who constitutes all other created union or oneness, according to this pleasure, and for what purposes, communications, and effects he pleases, may not establish a constitution whereby the natural posterity of Adam, proceeding from him, much as the buds and branches from the stock or root of a tree, should be treated as one with him, for the derivation, either of righteousness and communion in rewards, or of the loss of righteousness and consequent corruption and guilt." The children of Adam by their nature recapitulate his apostasy in time, so that his sin is "*truly* and *properly* theirs, and on that ground, God imputes it to them," and their children. Though it may "sit easier on the imagination" to limit the suffering of "poor little infants" to death in this world, it defies reason, because God imputes the whole of the sin not "some *little* part" of it. The very young share with the race one corrupt nature and one eternal hell. Imputation is identity writ large by the hand of God.

Infant damnation and other minor objections. Edwards returns to the question of infant damnation in the final chapter of Part IV only to dismiss it. If children have a negative virtue that renders them incapable of wicked acts, as Taylor claims, Edwards reminds him that a "young viper has a malignant nature, though incapable of doing a malignant action, and at present appearing a harmless creature." He dispatches eleven more objections as quickly, if somewhat less tartly: objections that original sin abrogates God's covenant with Noah; that it disparages divine goodness, violates the process of judgment, negates personal imputation, and contemns human nature; and that it promotes hatred (it teaches humility and "mutual *compassion*," Edwards replies), gloom ("'tis fit, it should" till salvation), sin ("on this head" see "my discourse" on the will), and celibacy (even children can learn faith: "I think, this may be answer enough to such a cavil"). To Taylor's objection that Christ "says not one word" about original sin in the Gospels, Edwards cites twenty texts that "plainly" imply it, beginning with Matt. 9:12, the verse on his title page. "But if after all, Christ did not speak of this doctrine often enough to suit Dr. Taylor, he might be asked, why he supposes Christ did no oftener, and no more plainly teach some of his (Dr. Taylor's) doctrines, which he so much insists on?"

And then in the "Conclusion," a handful of pages, Edwards takes the good doctor to task for his manner, for his distortion of Paul's words and the cunning of his own. Taylor shows "magisterial assurance," "dictatorial peremptoriness," and "high contempt" for the past and "old opinions and old expositions." Only now, "in this happy age of light and liberty," writes a scornful Edwards, can readers of Paul's epistles understand what the *"unlearned* and *shortsighted"* of ages past had only a hint. Taylor analyzes and criticizes until "holy Scripture is subtilized into a mere mist; or made to evaporate into a thin cloud, that easily puts on any shape." Exhausted, Edwards cries, "'Tis not in the nature and power of language, to afford sufficient defense against such an art, so abused," and leaves his readers to judge. A few pages earlier, he had left them another task, one somewhat more difficult to fulfill soon.

A Meditation on Virtue

Beauty and love, by definition. In the last lines of Part IV, Edwards had mentioned "many late writers" who argue that virtue is innate, that mankind has "a native bent" towards benevolence, and that such a natural tendency contravenes original sin. But by then he had run out of space, and so he had referred interested readers to his detailed reply, "a *Treatise on the Nature of True Virtue,* lying by me prepared for the press, which may ere long be exhibited to public view." Eight years would pass before it was published as one of two dissertations, the same year Samuel Hopkins published his life of Edwards, 1765.[20] The anonymous author of the preface—in all probability, Hopkins—thought the treatise more suited for "the learned and the inquisitive" than the common reader. Within half a dozen years, one learned reader found *True Virtue* uncommonly unorthodox; in another two years, Hopkins was back to defend it, and Edwards generally, against mounting criticism.[21] Yet it is Edwards at his least polemical, burdened by few agate notes and free of serial citations. It also happens to be Edwards at his most radical.

True Virtue is a meditation of sorts on the terms of the definition Edwards starts with: "True virtue most essentially consists in *benevolence to being in general.*" Virtue consists in beauty, not the beauty of nature, man, or mind—a flower, a face, a thought—but moral beauty, some act or habit of the heart that evokes praise. Beauty may be general or particular, that is, it may be a complete relationship to all parts or an incomplete relationship. Just as a few musical notes in tune with themselves may be harmonious, so measured by all notes in a tune, the same may be discordant. Virtue, even "the more considerable Deists" agree, also consists in love to being. Love may be either love of benevolence, a delight in being for its happiness; or love of complacence, a delight in being for its beauty. But if virtue consists in beauty as well as delight in beauty, then beauty is both subject and object of virtue, an absurdity. Thus the "primary object of virtuous love is being, simply considered."

It follows that if being is the first object of virtue, then that object which has the "most of being" deserves the greatest share of benevolence. The second object of virtuous love is benevolent being, benevolence attaching to benevolence. Such "pure" benevolence comprises "true moral or spiritual beauty," the principles and acts that unite to being in general. The degree of virtuous love will be in proportion to the "greatness of the benevolent being." That God is infinite being, infinitely beautiful, excellent, and glorious, "must necessarily" mean that all true virtue must "radically and essentially" consist in *love to God.*" All else is "secondary" or "inferior."

Love of God, love of self.   Unless founded upon love to God, love of any kind—of one another, family, neighbors, community, country, mankind—is "fundamentally and essentially defective." Love to a particular person or to "a private system" fails to account to infinite being and thus fails true virtue. Some moral philosophers, Francis Hutcheson among them, probably Edwards's principal source, mention God "so slightly" that their ethics turn secular on an inconsistency, for if true virtue consists "partly" of love to God, it must as a consequence of infinitude consist "chiefly" in it. "And therefore certainly, unless we will be Atheists, we must allow that true virtue does primarily and most essentially consist in a supreme love to God; and that where this is wanting, there can be no true virtue" or, for that matter, "true *grace*" or "real *holiness.*" The rest of the dissertation, three quarters of the text, explains what true virtue is not, and here, like *Freedom of the Will* before it and *Original Sin* after it, the argument hinges on the distinction between natural man and spiritual, first in matters of beauty and then, more extensively, in matters of love.

Natural and secondary beauty has to do with the "mutual consent and agreement of different things," inanimate or animate, in order, proportion, design, and the like, a Newtonian world of equilateral triangles and regular polygons; notes in harmony; colors and figures on chintz; "an ingenious complicated machine"; the levels of society; the symmetry of a human face; a sense of justice. These "numberless instances" of secondary beauty constitute an "analogy" to the primary and original beauty of the spiritual world, "images or shadows of divine things," Edwards called them years ago. Still, a man may not perceive them as such nor know virtue through his delight in them. Benevolence, Edwards remarks, has little to do with "a man's loving the taste of honey, or his being pleased with the smell of a rose."

In matters of love, Edwards rejects the notion of some moral philosophers—Hobbes, certainly—that all love arises from self-love. For him, self-love is simply an inferior sort, the amiable product of natural man. An "ambiguous" term at best, self-love means both a man's love of what he loves—the pleasure principle—and, more commonly, a man's love of his "confined self" or "private interest." His love of himself makes "him love love of himself" and thoroughly dominates his nature as God "constituted" it. And contrary to the imaginings of some moral philosophers, God has not "implanted in the hearts of all mankind" a sense out of which gratitude or anger grows, moral rose or belladonna. Edwards likens that kind of moral sense to secondary beauty in that it partakes of harmony or proportion only—"as they love us and do us good, we also should love them and do them good"—whether as private or public benevolence, of persons or traits, in art or reality. "Is there need of a great degree of subtlety and abstraction to make it out, that a child, who has heard and seen much of what is calculated strongly to fix an idea of the pernicious, deadly nature of the rattlesnake, should have an aversion to that species from self-love; so as to have a degree of this aversion and disgust excited by seeing even the picture of that animal?" Moral sense arises from self-love, strengthened through the "association of ideas" and "vastly heightened by education." Observes Edwards, glancing up from his Stockbridge desk, "anyone would be convinced, perhaps more effectually than in most other ways, if they had an opportunity of any considerable acquaintance with American savages and their children."

Unlike pure love, which implies acting "as though others were one with ourselves," self-love implies acting "as one with ourselves," acting in harmony with ourselves rather than in union with God, acting from a natural principle rather than a divine one. That often means acting inconsistently, which prompts an uneasy feeling within us, an "inward trouble" of conscience. And that, in turn, forces us to judge what "passes between us and others" and impels us to fit the punishment to the injury or the reward to the kindness by "a sense of desert." In these private acts, natural conscience parallels the spiritual sense, approving or condemning what it does, even though it lacks "a benevolent temper of mind" or a love to God. It "concurs" with His law, extends equally with it, and "joins its voice with it in every article." And to the extent that it is "disinterested," it is "the same" with the moral sense. By whatever name, as "an internal judge" it establishes within us "a clear sense" of vice or virtue.

Instincts and the uses of conscience. Some moral philosophers take other natural dispositions as sources and expressions of true virtue, but, Edwards points out, none of these natural dispositions share the general benevolence necessary to virtue. Instincts, expressed as natural affection, may resemble virtue in the caring of parents, the love between a man and a woman, or the pity for others in distress, but natural affection in "a private system" is inferior, "so long as it contains but an infinitely small part of universal existence." The "mutual" and "kind" love that "naturally" arises between the sexes, "sensitive pleasure" aside, does not arise from true virtue because it is "limited." Pity, "implanted" by God, is "very different" from true virtue because it is often mixed: "Men may pity others under exquisite torment, when yet they would have been grieved if they had seen their prosperity." That God designed these natural instincts for our preservation and "comfortable subsistence" will count for nothing at judgment: "in the world of punishment, there will be no such thing as a disposition to pity, in any case; as also no natural affection towards near relations, and no mutual affections between opposite sexes." As Edwards envisions the world, true virtue spins upon the bleak axis of original sin.

Still, these natural dispositions—conscience, parental affection, sexual love, pity, and gratitude, self-love itself—are "exceeding useful and necessary" to society, even though they fall short of general benevolence and "leave the divine Being out." Indeed, they are often mistaken for virtue (in both its primary and secondary operation) precisely because they share the "same denomination" and yield the "same effect," that is, restrain sin and encourage virtue, the closer they draw to "disinterested general benevolence." All these natural dispositions have their counterpart in true virtue, virtuous love of parents, of town or country, "Yea, and a virtuous love between the sexes, as there may be the influence of virtue mingled with instinct." In this, true virtue makes "gentler" the natural instincts, "softens and sweetens the mind."

In the last chapter, Edwards returns to the opening lines of his dissertation by way of definition, with a difference. Then, to "all excepting some sceptics," virtue meant "something beautiful"; now, virtue means "a certain kind of beautiful nature," but with this qualification, that the beautiful comes to us "immediately" in itself. If beauty is founded on "immediate sensation" and not on argument, then, Edwards asserts, "virtue is founded on sentiment, and not in reason." God gives this "inward" or spiritual sense of virtue to man by "absolute necessity," for to do so arbitrarily, as some claim, would be contrary to His temper and nature—His love of Himself—and contrary to the nature of things, the "correspondence and agreement" that informs the created world. So by necessity, natural conscience or the moral sense, though inferior to true virtue, is founded on similar sentiments. Further, this moral sense "chiefly governs" the language we use to express "our *sentiments*" of right and wrong and enables us, as God intends, to judge them. Edwards concludes (as might Emerson), "Mankind in general seem to suppose some general standard, or foundation in nature, for an universal consistence in the use of terms whereby they express moral good and evil."[22]

Summa Theologica, Part the Last

The trials of language. Of the four notes Edwards appended to *True Virtue* two refer to its companion piece, "the preceding discourse of God's end in creating the world."[23] Longer by half, that discourse also lies closer than *True Virtue* to Edwards's typical method of inquiry, the argument from reason buttressed by the argument from Scripture. In this instance, Edwards devotes fully half his text, the second of two chapters, to "what is to be learned from the Holy Scriptures" about the end of creation. He finds that "the great and last end of God's works which is so variously expressed in Scripture, is indeed but *one*; and this *one* end is most properly and comprehensively called, the glory of God." Reason, of course, bears that out.

Like its companion piece, *The End of Creation* dwells on definitions, the limits of reason, and the trials of language. Thus in a note about the phrase "*God's fulness,*" Edwards remarks that he uses it "partly because I know of no better phrase to be used in this general meaning," and at the end of the chapter on reason, he confesses to "a great imperfection in the expressions we use" to describe "the incomprehensibleness of those things that are divine." At the beginning of that chapter, he acknowledges that "it would be relying too much on reason" to determine the end of creation, especially "since God has given a revelation containing instructions concerning this matter." Still, in his introduction to the text, he sets out with definitions—with words and reason—and pursues their consequences as by an act of discovery.

At the start, Edwards distinguishes the chief end of a thing from its ultimate end, defining the first as the most valued end and the other as the end for its own sake. He illustrates one kind of difference with a journey—his?—for love and science.

Thus a man may go a journey partly to obtain the possession and enjoyment of a bride that is very dear to him, and partly to gratify his curiosity in looking in a telescope, or some new invented and extraordinary optic glass: both may be ends he seeks in his journey, and the one not properly subordinate or in order to another. One may not depend on another, and therefore both may be ultimate ends; but yet the obtaining his beloved bride may be his chief end, and the benefit of the optic glass, his inferior end. The former may be what he sets his heart vastly most upon, and so be properly the chief end of his journey.[24]

Other journeys help explain other distinctions among other ends, subordinate, consequential, original, first, and last. But at one point, Edwards invokes "some third being," neither God nor man, to determine how things fit into the whole existence and to judge the end of it. Such a perfectly wise and disinterested "arbiter" would determine that "the supreme and last end" of the universe, all its creatures and its events, should be God, "that every wheel, both great and small, in all its rotations, should move with a constant, invariable regard to him as the ultimate end of all; as perfectly and uniformly, as if the whole system were animated and directed by one common soul." The works of God regard Him so because God has "a supreme regard" for Himself.

In the beginning and in the end. A "fountain of infinite light," God emanates His fullness of good, diffuses His beauty and holiness, and "makes himself his end." That man loves and delights in Him did not move God to create him, even though His "diffusive disposition" moves Him to communicate His fullness to His creatures when they exist. "Therefore, to speak more strictly according to truth, we may suppose, that a disposition in God, as an original property of his nature, to an emanation of his own infinite fullness, was what excited him to create the world; and so that the emanation itself was aimed at by him as a last end of the creation." Still, God seeks our good because in seeking it He seeks Himself. It is "nothing but" an expression of the fullness of good that God delights in, and another reminder that the end for which God created the world is God.

The first texts cited as scriptural proof of that dictum come from Isaiah (44:6)—"I am the first, and I am the last"—and its New Tes-

tament rendering in Revelation (1:8)—"I am Alpha and Omega."
Though he suggests a dozen positions to argue the affair, Edwards returns, as he must, to these unambiguous words. Like the text that
occasioned his "new sense" of things—"Now unto the King eternal,
immortal, invisible, the only wise God, be honor and glory for ever
and ever" (1 Tim. 1:17)—these converge to the center of his being and
his belief, the absolute sovereignty of God. Then, in East Windsor,
the thunder he heard rejoiced him though it foretold an uncertain
weather of the soul. Now, in Stockbridge, he ends, waiting: "and yet
there never will come the moment, when it can be said, that now this
infinitely valuable good has been actually bestowed." For Edwards,
only the prospect really mattered.

Chapter Six
Misrepresentations Corrected

A hundred and ninety-five years after he delivered the commencement sermon there, Yale dedicated Jonathan Edwards College: "its men," a pictorial history of the university notes, "are called 'Spiders.'"[1] Twenty-five years later, Yale University Press published *Freedom of the Will*, the first volume of what would become the definitive edition of his work. Between times, Edwards's reputation swelled and shifted, driven by a spate of creative scholarship. Between 1932 and 1957, appeared representative selections (1935), the printed writings (1940), the standard biography (1940), *Images or Shadows of Divine Things* (1948), Perry Miller's provocative study (1949), reconstructed notebooks (1955), an awful novel (1957), and scores of articles; doctoral dissertations on him tripled.[2] Clearly it was time for "The Reappraisal of Edwards," as an essay in the *New England Quarterly* for 1957 put it, time, perhaps, to close the book on *Jonathan Edwards: The Fiery Puritan* (1930). There was more to him than spiders.[3]

In 1830, the Reverend Dr. Lyman Beecher wrote his son at Yale, "Next after the Bible, read and study Edwards." His wife would have none of it. On hearing *Sinners in the Hands of an Angry God,* she cried, "'Dr. Beecher, I shall not listen to another word of that slander on my Heavenly father!' and swept out of the room."[4] Much of the century fled with her. Doctrines like infant damnation and imputation were obnoxious to many believers of the time or irrelevant, and Edwards suffered abuse at their hands or, worse still, neglect. James Boswell, who had read *Freedom of the Will,* reported Dr. Johnson, who hadn't, as saying, "'All theory is against freedom of the will; all experience for it.'" A young Emerson—he was twenty at the time—questioned Edwards's logic in it; an old Mark Twain questioned his sanity: a "drunken lunatic," he wrote in 1902, a "resplendent intellect gone mad."[5] *Original Sin* fared no better than *Freedom of the Will*: "revolting," said one reader, "very revolting," added another a decade later. And Edwards's style, the subject of study and praise in our time, got scathing reviews in the years following his. The editor of a shortened

Religious Affections defended it because Edwards's "monstrous profusion of words" rendered his ideas "feeble" and "obscure," one of "the most remarkable specimens of bad writing" of his time.[6]

Not everyone grieved so. After all, abridged or not, *Religious Affections* was in fact published and, as its printing history shows, more than a dozen times after 1817, a manual and witness for nineteenth-century evangelicals.[7] At times, a more balanced, if still highly critical view, emerged, Leslie Stephen's influential piece for *Fraser's* in 1873, for example, or A. V. G. Allen's full-length study in 1889, a first: both remarked the tension in Edwards between mysticism and Calvinism.[8] And in one year, 1907, three important studies were published: on his role in New England Theology, his departure from Reformed theology (in Dutch), and his development as an American philosopher.[9] These investigations aside, there were only minor revisions of earlier attitudes, framed neatly enough by the Edwards entries in the eleventh and fourteenth editions of the *Britannica*: the assertion that Edwards was "the most influential thinker in America" (1910) yielded in twenty years to the question of his "potent" influence and his "perpendicular piety" (1929).[10] With the tricentennial of the Massachusetts Bay Colony at hand and the celebration of Harvard's founding hard upon it came a renewed interest in Puritanism that led inevitably to Edwards as its intellectual exemplar. In 1932, Harvard—and Columbia and Chicago—granted its first doctorate for a dissertation on Edwards, and a sustained effort of serious and disinterested inquiry began.

Perhaps more than any other, Perry Miller effected that inquiry. His Edwards, the Edwards of his persistent study, was "intellectually the most modern man of his age," a speculative philosopher "infinitely more" than a theologian, a "major" artist rather, a psychologist and a poet in the native tradition. History and typology, ethics and aesthetics, these were the proper study; Locke and Newton, not Calvin; his "inspired definitions," not his often "pathetic" answers; the "drama of his ideas," not the prose on his days.[11] In time, the eighteenth-century pastor came to dominate the twentieth-century intellectual historian, and, in time, Miller's labors came to dominate the labors of others. From 1965 to 1975, doctoral candidates in America produced fifty-seven dissertations about Edwards, concerning, among other things, his ideas of glory and grace, typology and teleology; his social and educational theories; continuities beyond Emerson and comparisons with Stoddard; studies of his rhetoric and his symbolic system and his style. A dozen books about him were published during the same period. One in 1966, "a reappraisal" of his theology, considered him "first and last" a Calvinist. By the eighties, the author of a considerable book on his moral thought would claim that "Edwards himself was no Lockean," that his theory of virtue cannot be "strictly identified with institutionalized Christianity."[12] The *New Yorker* for 24 March 1980 published a poem about him "awaiting winter visitors"; *Yankee* for October 1985, published another about Sarah "who unpinned texts" from his greatcoat.[13] And so it goes, and so for Americans the question of his importance to their history and their society, their religion and their thought, abides.

The old dualities that haunted Edwards from the start remain unresolved—mystic and rationalist, philosopher and theologian, poet of the divine and scourger of the wicked. On the road from Northampton to Stockbridge, older, weary of bickering, it's likely he never stopped to give it thought.

Notes and References

Preface

1. "Jonathan Edwards," *The New American Cyclopaedia* (New York: D. Appleton, 1859), 7:20.

2. Letter to Mrs. Jane Mecom, 28 July 1743; reprinted in *The Papers of Benjamin Franklin*, ed. Leonard W. Labaree (New Haven: Yale University Press, 1960), 2:385.

3. For a portrait of that time, see Richard Hofstadter, *America at 1750* (New York: Alfred A. Knopf, 1971).

4. Letter, 19 October 1757, in Samuel Hopkins, *The Life and Character of the Late Reverend Mr. Jonathan Edwards* (Boston: S. Kneeland, 1765); reprinted in David Levin, ed., *Jonathan Edwards: A Profile* (New York: Hill and Wang, 1969), 76.

Chapter 1

1. Hopkins, *Life and Character*, 24–39. Hopkins's comment (p. 24) introduces "Personal Narrative," which Hopkins calls "An Account of his Conversion, Experiences, and Religious Exercises, Given by Himself," a manuscript now lost. For critical comment on "Personal Narrative," see Daniel B. Shea, Jr., *Spiritual Autobiography in Early America* (Princeton: Princeton University Press, 1968), 182–233, and Sacvan Bercovitch, "The Ritual of American Autobiography: Edwards, Franklin, Thoreau," *Revue Français d'Etudes Américaines* 7 (May 1982): 139–50.

2. "Personal Narrative," 24–28.

3. Besides Hopkins, the chief sources for Edwards's life are Sereno Edwards Dwight, *Life of President Edwards* (New York: S. Converse, 1829), and Ola Elizabeth Winslow, *Jonathan Edwards, 1703–1758: A Biography* (New York: Macmillan Co., 1940). Both are quite valuable for the manuscript material they transcribe, Winslow the more reliable of the two. For an important psychological study, see Richard L. Bushman, "Jonathan Edwards as Great Man: Identity, Conversion, and Leadership in the Great Awakening," *Soundings* 52 (Spring 1969):15–46.

4. Reprinted in Winslow, *Jonathan Edwards*, 40–41.

5. "Personal Narrative," 24.

6. Reprinted in Winslow, *Jonathan Edwards*, 49–50.

7. Letter of 30 June 1719, quoted in Winslow, *Jonathan Edwards*, 60.

For the difficulties at Yale, see Richard Warch, *School of the Prophets: Yale College, 1701–1740* (New Haven: Yale University Press, 1973), 70–136.

8. See Edwards's letter to his father, 21 July 1719, reprinted in Dwight, *President Edwards,* 31–32. For a discussion of the curriculum at Harvard (and Yale), see Samuel Eliot Morrison, *Three Centuries at Harvard, 1636–1936* (Cambridge: Harvard University Press, 1936), 29–31; Wallace E. Anderson's introduction to *Scientific and Philosophical Writings, The Works of Jonathan Edwards,* (New Haven: Yale University Press, 1980), 6:11–16; and Norman Fiering, *Jonathan Edwards's Moral Thought and Its British Context* (Chapel Hill: University of North Carolina Press, 1981), 14–33. Edwards recorded books read or to be read in his "catalogue": see Thomas H. Johnson, "Jonathan Edwards' Background of Reading," *Publications of the Colonial Society of Massachusetts* 28 (December 1931):193–222. When Edwards read Locke remains a question, but almost an answered one: compare Hopkins, *Life and Character,* 5–6, Anderson, *Scientific Writings,* 16–26, and Fiering, *Edwards's Moral Thought,* 35–40, on whether he was thirteen or seventeen.

9. Letter of 24 July 1719, quoted in Winslow, *Jonathan Edwards,* 66 and 345.

10. Undated letter, quoted in Winslow, *Jonathan Edwards,* 67–68.

11. Letter of 1 March 1721, reprinted in Winslow, *Jonathan Edwards,* 70–72.

12. "Personal Narrative," 30.

13. For an account of Edwards's stay, see Wilson H. Kimnach, "Jonathan Edwards' Early Sermons: New York, 1722–1723," *Journal of Presbyterian History* 55 (Fall 1977):255–66.

14. "Personal Narrative," 31–32.

15. Dwight, *President Edwards,* reprints all seventy "Resolutions" (68–73) and the "Diary" (76–94, 99–106); both manuscripts are now lost.

16. Reprinted in Dwight, *President Edwards,* 114–15.

17. *George Whitefield's Journals,* ed. Iain Murray (London: Banner of Truth Trust, 1960), 477.

18. Letter of 22 June 1748, reprinted in *Jonathan Edwards: Representative Selections,* ed. Clarence H. Faust and Thomas H. Johnson (New York: American Book Co., 1935), 384.

19. Hopkins, *Life and Character,* 40.

20. *God Glorified* (Boston: S. Kneeland and T. Green, 1731). Thomas Prince and William Cooper, "To the Reader," ii.

21. *A Faithful Narrative* (1737); reprinted in *Jonathan Edwards: The Great Awakening,* ed. C. C. Goen, *The Works of Jonathan Edwards* (New Haven: Yale University Press, 1972), 4:149.

22. Letter of 30 May 1735, reprinted in Faust and Johnson, *Representative Selections,* 83.

23. Dwight, *President Edwards,* 139–140.

24. *Discourses on Various Important Subjects* (Boston: S. Kneeland and T. Green, 1738). Edwards remarks on these matters in his preface to the text, iii–iv. It is about this time that Edwards delivered a series of sermons that became (posthumously) *A History of the Work of Redemption* (1774) and *Charity and Its Fruits* (1852); he probably composed "Personal Narrative" (1765) as well.

25. *The Autobiography of Benjamin Franklin*, ed. Leonard W. Labaree et al. (New Haven: Yale University Press, 1964), 177.

26. *George Whitefield's Journals*, 477.

27. Hopkins, *Life and Character*, 39 and 47–48.

28. Quoted in Perry Miller, *Jonathan Edwards* (New York: William Sloane Associates, 1949), 51.

29. Rev. Stephen William (Longmeadow, Mass.), manuscript diary; reprinted in Oliver William Means, *A Sketch of the Strict Congregational Church at Enfield, Connecticut* (Hartford: Hartford Seminary Press, 1899), 19.

30. *Sinners in the Hands of an Angry God* (Boston: S. Kneeland and T. Green, 1741), 25.

31. These are, in order, *Resort and Remedy* (1741); *Great Concern* (1743); *True Excellency* (1744); *Copies of the Two Letters* (1745); *An Expostulatory Letter* (1745); and *The Church's Marriage* (1746).

32. For a study of the shift in clerical authority in Northampton, see Patricia J. Tracy, *Jonathan Edwards, Pastor: Religion and Society in Eighteenth-Century Northampton* (New York: Hill & Wang, 1980), and, more generally, Emory Elliot, *Revolutionary Writers: Literature and Authority in the New Republic, 1725–1810* (New York: Oxford University Press, 1982), 19–54.

33. Letter of 26 March 1744, reprinted in Winslow, *Jonathan Edwards*, 217. For further evidence see Leonard T. Grant, "A Preface to Jonathan Edwards' Financial Difficulties," *Journal of Presbyterian History* 45 (March 1967):27–32.

34. Thomas H. Johnson, "Jonathan Edwards and the 'Young Folks' Bible,'" *New England Quarterly* 5 (January 1932): 37–54.

35. Hopkins, *Life and Character*, 54.

36. See George Leon Walker, "Jonathan Edwards and the Half-Way Covenant," *New Englander* 43 (September 1884): 601–14; and John F. Jamieson, "Jonathan Edwards's Change of Position on Stoddardeanism," *Harvard Theological Review* 74 (January 1981): 79–99.

37. Hopkins, *Life and Character*, 56.

38. Dwight, *President Edwards*, 202. See also Norman Petit, "Prelude to Mission: Brainerd's Expulsion from Yale," *New England Quarterly* 59 (March 1986):28–50.

39. Quoted in Winslow, *Jonathan Edwards*, 237.

40. Letter of 31 August 1748; reprinted in Dwight, *President Edwards*, 252.

41. Reprinted in Dwight, *President Edwards,* 313–99; the quotations are found on pp. 315, 316, 318, 319, 324, 327, 339, 368, 389, and 390.

42. Letter of 2 April 1750, reprinted in Dwight, *President Edwards,* 296.

43. Hopkins, *Life and Character,* 61.

44. Dwight, *President Edwards,* 125; for a detailed account, see Charles Edwin Jones, "The Impolitic Mr. Edwards: The Personal Dimension of the Robert Breck Affair," *New England Quarterly* 51 (March 1978):64–79.

45. Dwight, *President Edwards,* 400.

46. Hopkins, *Life and Character,* 61. C. C. Goen puts the figure at 230 to 23; see *Works* (Yale), 4:87.

47. *Farewell Sermon* (1751); reprinted in *The Works of President Edwards,* ed. Samuel Austin (Worcester, Mass.: Isaiah Thomas, 1808), 1:101–41; the quotations are found on pp. 110, 125–26, 130, 135, and 140–41.

48. Letter of 5 July 1750, reprinted in Dwight, *President Edwards,* 412–13.

49. Letter of 15 November 1750, reprinted in Dwight, *President Edwards,* 415–18.

50. Hopkins, *Life and Character,* 63–65.

51. Letter of 18 November 1754; reprinted in Faust and Johnson, *Representative Selections,* 392–401; the quotations are found on pp. 393–95, 397, and 400–401.

52. Reprinted in *Works* (1808), 1:343–515; the pause occurs on p. 444.

53. Dwight, *President Edwards,* 507. Ephraim Williams (the younger) founder of Williams College, commented in a letter of 2 May 1751, "I am sorry that a head so full of Divinity should be so empty of Politics." Reprinted in Arthur Latham Perry, *Origins of Williamstown* (New York: Charles Scribner's Sons, 1896), 639–40.

54. Letter of 27 January 1752; reprinted in Dwight, *President Edwards,* 486. Edwards acknowledges his own inadequacies when he sends his son Jonathan, aged nine, to learn the language of the Iroquois by living among them (Dwight, 544).

55. *True Grace* (1753) was preached before the New York Synod meeting in Newark, N.J., 28 September 1752.

56. Letter of 5 July 1750; reprinted in Dwight, *President Edwards,* 411.

57. Letter of 7 July 1752; reprinted in Dwight, *President Edwards,* 497.

58. Reprinted in Dwight, *President Edwards,* 533.

59. Letter of 15 April 1755; reprinted in Dwight, *President Edwards,* 546.

60. Reprinted in Hopkins, *Life and Character,* 74–78.

61. Hopkins, *Life and Character,* 78.

62. Hopkins, *Life and Character,* 79–80.

63. Quoted in Winslow, *Jonathan Edwards,* 319.

64. Quoted in Hopkins, *Life and Character,* 81.

65. Letter of 3 April 1758; reprinted in Dwight, *President Edwards,* 580–81.

66. Edwards Amasa Park, ed., "Jonathan Edwards' Last Will, and the Inventory of his Estate," *Bibliotheca Sacra* 33 (July 1876):438–47.

Chapter 2

1. Hopkins, *Life and Character,* 28.

2. Reprinted in *Scientific and Philosophical Writings,* ed. Wallace E. Anderson, *The Works of Jonathan Edwards* (New Haven: Yale University Press, 1980), 6:219–95. Entries on thunder and lightning appear on pp. 222–23, 282–83, and 294. Anderson's general introduction (1–143) and headnotes (147–53; 173–91; 296–97; and 394–95) are particularly useful.

3. *Works* (Yale), 6:396–97.

4. Isaac Newton, *Opticks* (London: William Innys, 1730), 381. Edwards probably read the 1706 edition.

5. *Works* (Yale), 6:161.

6. *Works* (Yale), 6:223.

7. "Diary," 12 September 1723; reprinted in Dwight, *President Edwards,* 84.

8. *Images or Shadows of Divine Things,* ed. Perry Miller (New Haven: Yale University Press, 1948), 71.

9. Reprinted in *Works* (Yale) 6:154–62. Edwards probably wrote it between 1719 and 1720 (Anderson, *Scientific Writing,* 147–50) rather than in 1715 (Egbert Coffin Smyth, "The Flying Spider—Observations by Jonathan Edwards When a Boy," *Andover Review* 13 [January 1890]: 1–19).

10. *Works* (Yale), 6:163–69.

11. But there is a mention of his father. Judge Dudley cites "The Reverend Mr. Edwards of Windsor" as the source for a report on a pumpkin harvest in 1669, noted in an article published by the Royal Society (1724) and reprinted in part in *Works* (Yale) 6:163, n. 3.

12. "Juvenile Observations of President Edwards on Spiders," *American Journal of Science and Arts* 21 (January 1832): 109–15. For a contrary view, see David S. Wilson, "The Flying Spider," *Journal of the History of Ideas* 32 (July 1971): 447–58. For a general assessment of Edwards as scientist, see Clarence H. Faust, "Jonathan Edwards as a Scientist," *American Literature* 1 (January 1930): 393–404; Rufus O. Suter, "An American Pascal: Jonathan Edwards," *Scientific American* 68 (May 1949): 338–42; and Anderson, *Scientific Writings,* 37–52.

13. *Works* (Yale), 6:193.

14. *Works* (Yale), 6:196–201.

15. *Works* (Yale), 6:219–95.

16. The four papers are "Of the Rainbow," *Works* (Yale), 6:298–301; "Of Light Rays," 6:302–4; "Beauty of the World," 6:305–6; and "Wisdom in the Contrivance of the World," 6:307–10.

17. *Works* (Yale), 6:208–18.

18. On the development of Edwards's philosophical speculations, see Leroy Adam Jones, *Early American Philosophers* (New York: MacMillan Co., 1898), 46–80; I. Woodbridge Riley, *American Philosophy: The Early Schools* (New York: Dodd, Mead & Co., 1907), 126–87; Harvey Gates Townsend, *Philosophical Ideas in the United States* (New York: American Book Co., 1934), 35–62; John E. Smith, "Jonathan Edwards as Philosophical Theologian," *Review of Metaphysics* 30 (December 1976):306–24; Elizabeth Flower and Murray G. Murphey, *A History of Philosophy in America* (New York: G. P. Putnam's Sons, 1977), 1:137–99; Bruce Kuklick, *Churchmen and Philosophers from Jonathan Edwards to John Dewey* (New Haven: Yale University Press, 1985), 15–42; and Anderson, *Scientific Writings*, 52–136.

19. No. 26 of the long series in "Things to be Considered and Written Fully About"; reprinted in *Works* (Yale), 6:235.

20. Reprinted in *Works* (Yale), 6:202–7.

21. Reprinted in *Works* (Yale), 6:332–93. For Edwards on excellency, see pp. 332–38 and 364; for the ideal world, pp. 343–44 and 351; for the reality of God, pp. 353–57. Leon Howard provides a running commentary on these and other matters in his *"The Mind" of Jonathan Edwards: A Reconstructed Text* (Berkeley: University of California Press, 1963).

22. Though some of the "Miscellanies" have been reprinted, most notably by Harvey Gates Townsend, ed., *The Philosophy of Jonathan Edwards from His Private Notebooks* (Eugene: University of Oregon Press, 1955), the complete text awaits Thomas A. Schafer's edition for the Yale Edwards.

23. *Works* (Yale), 6:370–71.

24. For Newton's influence, see James H. Tufts, "Edwards and Newton," *Philosophical Review* 49 (November 1940): 609–22; for Locke's influence, a more disputed claim, see Miller, *Jonathan Edwards*, 52–67 and 235–40. Over the years, scholars have offered a variety of other influences on Edwards's scientific and philosophical thought, among them (alphabetically): Antoine Arnauld (Leon Howard, "The Creative Imagination of a College Rebel: Jonathan Edwards' Undergraduate Writings," *Early American Literature* 5 (Winter 1971): 50–56); George Berkeley (Georges Lyon, *L'Idéalisme en Angleterre au XVIIIe Siècle* [Paris: Ancienne Librarie Germer Baillière, 1888] 406–39); Francis Burgersdycke (William S. Morris, "The Genius of Jonathan Edwards," in *Reinterpretation in American Church History*, ed. Jerald C. Brauer (Chicago: Chicago University Press, 1968), 29–65); Arthur Collier (John Henry MacCracken, "The Sources of Jonathan Edwards's Idealism," *Philosophical Review* 11 (January 1902): 26–42); Ralph Cudworth (Clarence Gohdes, "Aspects of

Idealism in Early New England, *Philosophical Review* 39 (November 1930): 537–55); Nicolas Malebranche (Norman Fiering, *Jonathan Edwards's Moral Thought and Its British Context* (Chapel Hill: University of North Carolina Press, 1981), 40–45 and 341–45); and Henry More (Anderson, *Scientific Writings,* 23–24 and 57–63).

25. Hopkins (*Life and Character,* 5–6) reports that Edwards told this to a group of friends shortly before his death.

26. John Locke, *An Essay Concerning Human Understanding,* ed. Peter H. Nidditch (Oxford: The Clarendon Press, 1975), II.1.2–4 (104–6). Edwards probably read the second edition, 1694; see Anderson, *Scientific Writings,* 26, n. 8.

27. Edwards has in mind Locke's *Essay* II.27.9–17 (335–41) in the first instance; and Locke's *Essay* II.21.31–40 (250–58) in the second.

28. The limits of Locke's influence are defined in Claude A. Smith, "Jonathan Edwards and 'The Way of Ideas,'" *Harvard Theological Review* 59 (April 1966): 153–73; Paul Helm, "John Locke and Jonathan Edwards: A Reconsideration," *Journal of the History of Philosophy* 7 (January 1969): 51–61; Sang Hyun Lee, "Jonathan Edwards' Theory of the Imagination," *Michigan Academician* 5 (Fall 1972): 233–41; and David Laurence, "Jonathan Edwards, John Locke, and the Canon of Experience," *Early American Literature* 15 (Fall 1980): 107–23.

29. For an examination of "Notes on the Apocalypse" and citations in "Notes in Scripture," see Stephen J. Stein's introduction to his edition of *Apocalyptic Writings, The Works of Jonathan Edwards* (New Haven: Yale University Press, 1977), 5:1–93.

30. Reprinted in Dwight, *President Edwards,* 70.

31. Stein, *Apocalyptic Writings,* 49, n. 9.

Chapter 3

1. *God Glorified* (Boston: S. Kneeland and T. Green, 1731), i–ii; reprinted in *Works* (1808), 7:466–85.

2. *Distinguishing Marks* (Boston: S. Kneeland and T. Green, 1741), i–xviii.

3. *Humble Inquiry* (Boston: S. Kneeland, 1749), vi.

4. Hopkins, *Life and Character,* 76.

5. Full-scale appraisals of Edwards and his work include Alexander V. G. Allen, *Jonathan Edwards* (Boston: Houghton Mifflin, 1889); Henry Bamford Parkes, *Jonathan Edwards: The Fiery Puritan* (New York: Minton, Balch, 1930); Perry Miller, *Jonathan Edwards* (New York: William Sloane, 1949); Alfred Owen Aldridge, *Jonathan Edwards* (New York: Washington Square Press, 1964); Conrad Cherry, *The Theology of Jonathan Edwards* (Garden City, N.Y.: Doubleday, 1966); Edward H. Davidson, *Jonathan Edwards: The*

Narrative of a Puritan Mind (Boston: Houghton Mifflin, 1966); Harold P. Simonson, *Jonathan Edwards: Theologian of the Heart* (Grand Rapids, Mich.: William B. Eerdmans, 1974); and William J. Scheick, *The Writings of Jonathan Edwards: Theme, Motif, and Style* (College Station: Texas A&M University Press, 1975). Shorter but still quite useful are Clarence H. Faust and Thomas H. Johnson, *Jonathan Edwards: Representative Selections* (New York: American Book, 1935), xi–cxvii; and Elizabeth Flower and Murray G. Murphey, *A History of Philosophy in America* (New York: G. P. Putnam, 1977), 1:137–99.

6. See Josephine Piercy, *Studies in Literary Types in Seventeenth-Century America (1607–1710)* (New Haven: Yale University Press, 1939), 155–67; and Babette May Levy, *Preaching in the First Half Century of New England History* (Hartford: American Society of Church History, 1945), 81–97.

7. The citations in order are 2 Pet. 1:4 and Heb. 10:4 in the first paragraph; John 4:14, John 7:38–39, Rev. 22:1, 2 Cor. 1:22, 2 Cor. 5:5, and Eph. 1:13–14 in the second; Matt. 7:11, Luke 11:13, Gal. 3:13–14, Luke 29:49, Eph. 1:33, and Acts 2:13 in the third; and Rom. 11:36 and 1 Cor. 8:6 in the last. *Works* (1808), 7:477–80.

8. For Edwards's biblicism, see Stephen J. Stein, "Quest for a Spiritual Sense: The Biblical Hermeneutics of Jonathan Edwards," *Harvard Theological Review* 70 (January 1977): 99–113; John H. Gerstner, "Jonathan Edwards and the Bible," *Tenth, an Evangelical Quarterly* 9 (October 1979): 1–71; and Samuel T. Logan, Jr., "The Hermeneutics of Jonathan Edwards," *Westminster Theological Journal* 43 (Fall 1980): 79–96.

9. See Annette Kolodny, "Imagery in the Sermons of Jonathan Edwards," *Early American Literature* 7 (Fall 1972): 172–82. The metaphoric structure of the sermons forms the basis of a book-length study (in Italian), Marcella DeNichilo, *Realtà e immagine: L'estetica nei sermoni di Jonathan Edwards* (L'Aquila: L. U. Japadre, 1980).

10. Yet more than a century after his death his views on the trinity set off a round of suspicion, charges of suppressed texts and outright heterodoxy, the dreary stuff of paper wars and theological claimants. With the publication of a manuscript essay on the trinity on the bicentennial of his birth, Edwards's orthodoxy was affirmed; it still is. For a short history of the controversy, see Richard D. Pierce, "A Suppressed Edwards Manuscript on the Trinity," *Crane Review* 1 (Winter 1959): 66–80; for his orthodoxy, see the introduction to Paul Helm's edition of Edwards's *Treatise on Grace and Other Posthumously Published Writings* (London: James Clarke, 1971), 1–23. The quotation is found in *Works* (1808), 7:481.

11. See Wilson H. Kimnach, "Jonathan Edwards' Sermon Mill," *Early American Literature* 10 (Fall 1975): 167–77, on Edwards's practice of revision.

12. The dates cited in the text are those given by Edwards's son and namesake, himself a minister and college president, in his edition of fifteen of his father's sermons, though the dates of some, as he explains, remain

unknown. "Those I suppose were written before the year 1733, when the author was thirty years of age; as in that year he began to date his sermons, and all written after that, appear to be dated." *Sermons On the Following Subjects* (Hartford: Hudson and Goodwin, 1780), v. Samuel Hopkins appends *Sermons On Various Important Subjects* to his life of Edwards (1765); others appear in *Practical Sermons, Never Before Published* (Edinburgh: M. Gray, 1788), transcribed by his son. Wilson H. Kimnach is preparing—and dating—the manuscript sermons for the Yale Edwards: see John E. Smith, "Summary Report of the Progress of *The Works of Jonathan Edwards,*" *Early American Literature* 14 (Winter 1979): 352–53.

13. The sermons are reprinted (in order) in *Works* (1829), 6:58–68, 304–13, 381–413, 414–23, and 498–516.

14. *Sermons* (1780), 221–82; see *Works* (1808), 8:262, 272, and 277.

15. *Sermons* (1788), 343–85; see *Works* (1829), 6:549.

16. *Sermons* (1788), 133–50; see *Works* (1829), 6:379.

17. *Sermons* (1788), 260–82, and *Sermons* (1765), 165–252; reprinted in *Works* (1829), 6:466–85 and 7:66–114.

18. "The true Christian's Life, a Journey towards Heaven" (also called "The Christian Pilgrim"), *Sermons* (1765), 253–79; see *Works* (1808), 7:217.

19. "Great Care necessary, lest we live in some way of Sin," the substance of four sermons, *Sermons* (1788), 86–132; see *Works* (1808), 8:83 and 106.

20. *A Divine and Supernatural Light,* reprinted in *Works* (1808), 8:290–312; see pp. 294–97 for what the light is not, pp. 297–312 for what it is.

21. The three views are probably best represented by David Lyttle, "The Sixth Sense of Jonathan Edwards," *Church Quarterly Review* 167 (January 1966): 50–59; Ron Loewinsohn, "Jonathan Edwards' Opticks: Images and Metaphors in Some of His Major Works," *Early American Literature* 8 (Spring 1973): 21–32; and Terrence Erdt, "The Calvinist Psychology of the Heart and 'Sense' of Jonathan Edwards," *Early American Literature* 13 (Fall 1978): 165–80. Perry Miller, of course, had set the terms of the debate: see his *Jonathan Edwards,* 44–68.

22. The remarks are found in *Faithful Narrative* in *Works* (Yale), 4:147; the sermons, in *Works* (1808), 7:422–37; *Works* (1829), 6:486–97; *Works* (1808), 8:129–52; and *Works* (1829), 8:305–19.

23. *Discourses on Various Important Subjects* (Boston: S. Kneeland and T. Green, 1738); see Edwards's preface, i–vi.

24. The part justification plays in Edwards's theology generally, in the Northampton revivals, and in the Stockbridge years is dealt with, respectively, in Conrad Cherry, *Theology of Jonathan Edwards,* 90–106; Mary Foster, "Theological Debate in a Revival Setting: Hampshire County in the Great Awakening," *Fides et Historia* 6 (Spring 1974):31–47; and Thomas Schafer, "Jonathan Edwards and Justification by Faith," *Church History* 20 (December

1951): 55–67. The sermon itself is found in *Discourses*, 1–130; see *Works* (1808), 7:13–20 and 119 for Edwards's definition and verbal analysis.

25. *Discourses*, 131–72; see *Works* (1829), 5:465–75 especially.

26. *Discourses*, 173–91; see *Works* (1808), 7:319.

27. *Faithful Narrative* in *Works* (Yale), 4:168. The sermon (*Discourses*, 192–243) was a particular favorite of the public as well: it was reprinted a half-dozen times from 1773 to 1814.

28. Compare *Works* (1808), 7:128 and 7:340–46.

29. *Discourses*, 244–86; see *Works* (1808), 7:295 and 307.

30. *Sermons* (1780), 73–92; see *Works* (1808), 7:465.

31. *Sermons* (1788), 247–59; see *Works* (1829), 6:464–66.

32. The 30 May letter is reprinted in Faust and Johnson, *Representative Selections*, 73–83; the 3 June postscript, 83–84; the sermon "The sole consideration," *Sermons* (1788), 39–53, is reprinted in *Works* (1829), 6:293–303.

33. The title is that of the first American edition (Boston: S. Kneeland, T. Green, and D. Henchman, 1738), the third, in fact, counting Colman's abridgement of 1736 and the London (and Edinburgh) edition of 1737. The British title confounds geography, setting the revivals *in Northampton and the Neighbouring Towns and Villages of New-Hampshire in New-England*. However, the text here is that of the London edition, which Edwards corrected; C. C. Goen collated it with the American edition for the fourth volume of the Yale Edwards: *The Great Awakening* (New Haven: Yale University Press, 1972), 4:144–211. The preface to the first edition appears in *Works* (Yale), 4:130–37; the preface to the third edition, 138–42; and the attestation of ministers, 143.

34. For an account of the provenance of the text and the correspondence, see Anne Stokely Pratt, *Isaac Watts and His Gifts of Books to Yale College* (New Haven: Yale University Press, 1938), 32–47; and C. C. Goen, *The Great Awakening*, 32–46.

35. Compare the opening of the letters in Faust and Johnson, *Representative Selections*, 73, and *Works* (Yale), 4:144–47.

36. *Works* (Yale), 4:148–51 and 158.

37. See Edward S. Morgan, *Visible Saints: The History of a Puritan Idea* (New York: New York University, 1963); the phrase appears on p. 70.

38. For a general view of the "certain method," the traditional model of preparation, see Norman Petit, *The Heart Prepared: Grace and Conversion in Puritan Life* (New Haven: Yale University Press, 1966); for contending views of Edwards's model, see John H. and Jonathan Neil Gerstner, "Edwardsean Preparation for Salvation," *Westminster Theological Journal* 42 (Fall 1979): 5–71; David Laurence, "Jonathan Edwards, Solomon Stoddard, and the Preparationist Model of Conversion," *Harvard Theological Review* 72 (July 1979): 267–83. Edwards's account is found in *Works* (Yale), 4:160–66 and 176–85.

39. For the first, see *Works* (Yale), 4:191–99; for the second, 4:199–205.

40. *Works* (Yale), 4:206–11.

41. The first sermon, *Sermons* (1788), 39–53, is reprinted in *Works* (1829), 6:293–303; the second, *Sermons* (1788), 67–85, is reprinted in *Works* (1808), 8:44–65; the third, *Sermons* (1788), 26–38, is reprinted in *Works* (1808), 8:24–43.

42. In order, *Sermons* (1780), 57–71; see *Works* (1808), 7:450; *Sermons* (1765), 104–64, see *Works* (1808), 7:176 and 207; *Works* (1829), 8:70–104; and *Selected Sermons of Jonathan Edwards,* ed. Harry Norman Gardiner (New York: MacMillan, 1904), 64–77.

43. *Works* (1829), 8:428 and 431.

44. *Sermons* (1765), 24–58; see *Works* (1808), 7:150–51 and 155.

45. *Sermons* (1765), 13, 22, and 23.

46. *Charity and Its Fruits* (London: James Nisbet, 1852). Tryon Edwards observes that in his preface, iv.

47. *Charity and Its Fruits,* 297.

48. *Works* (1808), 7:396–421 and 8:461–80.

49. *A History of Redemption* (Edinburgh: W. Gray, 1774), vii–xi. The *History* is reprinted in *Works* (1808), 2:3–392. As an historian Edwards gets mixed reviews: See Peter Gay, *A Loss of Mastery: Puritan Historians in Colonial America* (Berkeley: University of California Press, 1966), 88–117; William J. Scheick, "The Grand Design: Jonathan Edwards' *History of the Work of Redemption,*" *Eighteenth Century Studies* 8 (Spring 1975): 300–14; and John F. Wilson, "Jonathan Edwards as Historian," *Church History* 46 (March 1977): 5–18.

50. Hopkins, *Life and Character,* 76–77.

51. *Works* (1808), 2:13–17 and 40.

52. *Works* (1808), 2:18 and 50.

53. See *Typology in Early American Literature,* ed. Sacvan Bercovitch (Amherst: University of Massachusetts Press, 1972); and Mason I. Lowance, Jr., *The Language of Canaan: Metaphor and Symbol in New England from the Puritans to the Transcendentalists* (Cambridge: Harvard University Press, 1980). The image is found in *Works* (1808), 2:48.

54. *Images or Shadows of Divine Things,* 109.

55. *Works* (1808), 2:284 and 308.

56. *Works* (1808), 2:382–83.

57. For American millennial hope, religious and then political, see Ernest Lee Tuveson, *Redeemer Nation: the Idea of America's Millennial Role* (Chicago: University of Chicago Press, 1968); James West Davidson, *The Logic of Millennial Thought: Eighteenth-Century New England* (New Haven: Yale University Press, 1977); and Nathan O. Hatch, *The Sacred Cause of Liberty: Republican Thought and the Millennium in Revolutionary New England* (New Haven: Yale University Press, 1977).

58. *Works* (1808), 2:354. On the question of the timing of the apocalypse, see Perry Miller, "The End of the World," *William and Mary Quarterly*

3rd ser. 8 (April 1951): 171–91; and Stephen J. Stein, "A Notebook on the Apocalypse by Jonathan Edwards," *William and Mary Quarterly* 3rd ser. 29 (October 1972): 623–34.

    59. *Sermons* (1788), 1–25; see *Works* (1808), 8:10–11, 22, and 27.

Chapter 4

    1. The literature on the Great Awakening is extensive, Edwards's role in it only a little less so. See, for example, Joseph Tracy, *The Great Awakening: A History of the Revival of Religion in the Time of Edwards and Whitefield* (Boston: Tappan and Dennet, 1842); Perry Miller, "Jonathan Edwards and the Great Awakening," in *America in Crisis,* ed. Daniel Aaron (New York: Alfred A. Knopf, 1952), 3–19; Edwin Scott Gaustad, *The Great Awakening in New England* (New York: Harper and Brothers, 1957); Alan Heimert, *Religion and the American Mind from the Great Awakening to the Revolution* (Cambridge: Harvard University Press, 1966); and C. C. Goen, "Editor's Introduction," to *The Great Awakening, The Works of Jonathan Edwards* (New Haven: Yale University Press, 1972), 4:1–95.

    2. *Sermons* (1765), 59–103; see *Works* (1829), 7:16 and 25. According to Dwight, Edwards also preached "The Character of Paul an Example to Christians" (Phil. 3:17) in February; reprinted, 8:123–58.

    3. *Sermons* (1780), 111–42; see *Works* (1808), 8:220.

    4. *Sermons* (1788), 321–44; reprinted in *Works* (1808), 8:481–506.

    5. *Sermons* (1780), 7–36; see *Works* (1829), 6:15–16.

    6. *Sermons* (1788), 224–46; see *Works* (1808), 8:159, 161, 167–68, and 172–73.

    7. *Works* (1829), 8:256–57 and 269.

    8. *Sermons* (1780), 143–69; see *Works* (1808), 7:377–78 for images of debt and rebellion; 7:387–88 for hell-fire; and 7:383–84 and 392–95 for hands.

    9. *Sinners in the Hands of an Angry God* (Boston: S. Kneeland and T. Green, 1741); reprinted in *Works* (1808), 7:486–502. As befits its fame, the sermon has been looked at rather closely: see, among others, Edwin H. Cady, "The Artistry of Jonathan Edwards," *New England Quarterly* 22 (March 1949): 61–72; Robert Lee Stuart, "Jonathan Edwards at Enfield: 'And Oh the Cheerfulness and Pleasantness. . . .' ," *American Literature* 48 (March 1976): 46–59; and Thomas J. Steele and Eugene R. Delay, "Vertigo in History: The Threatening Tactility of 'Sinners in the Hands of an Angry God,'" *Early American Literature* 18 (Winter 1983): 242–56.

    10. *Works* (1808), 7:487–89 and 491.

    11. *Works* (1808), 7:494–95.

    12. *Works* (1808), 7:496–97; compare 7:488 and 493.

    13. This paragraph, omitted from *Works* (1808), is restored in *Works* (1829), 7:175.

14. Benjamin Trumbull, *A Complete History of Connecticut, Civil and Ecclesiastical* (New Haven: Maltboy, Goldsmith, 1818), 2:145. Other eyewitness accounts can be found in Oliver William Means, *A Sketch of the Strict Congregational Church at Enfield, Connecticut* (Hartford: Hartford Seminary Press, 1899), 15–24; and Alexander Medlicott, Jr., "In the Wake of Mr. Edwards's 'Most Awakening' Sermon at Enfield," *Early American Literature* 15 (Winter 1980):217–21.

15. *Resort and Remedy* (Boston: G. Rogers, 1741); see *Works* (1808), 8:404–6.

16. *Distinguishing Marks* (Boston: S. Kneeland and T. Green, 1741); reprinted in *Works* (Yale), 4:215–88. For a contemporary reply to the sermon, see William Rand, *The Late Religious Commotions in New-England Considered* (Boston: Green, Bushell, and Allen, 1743).

17. *Works* (Yale), 4:231–32.

18. See *Works* (Yale), 4:228–48 for the negative signs; 4:250–59 for the positive ones.

19. *Works* (Yale), 4:267.

20. *Works* (Yale), 4:276–85.

21. Charles Chauncy, *Seasonable Thoughts* (Boston: Rogers and Fowle, 1743). The points of contention between Chauncy and Edwards are dealt with in Edward M. Griffin, *Old Brick: Charles Chauncy of Boston, 1705–1787* (Minneapolis: University of Minnesota Press, 1980), 37–46 and 78–88; and C. C. Goen's introduction, *Works* (Yale), 4:80–83. For an earlier analogue, see Norman S. Fiering, "Will and Intellect in the New England Mind," *William and Mary Quarterly* 3d ser. 29 (October 1972): 515–58.

22. *Some Thoughts* (Boston: S. Kneeland and T. Green, 1743). Reprinted in *Works* (Yale), 4:291–530, it is divided in five parts: I, 293–347; II, 348–83; III, 384–408; IV, 409–95; and V, 496–530. The first edition was published in 1743, not 1742 as the title page indicates; see C. C. Goen's introduction, 65.

23. *Works* (Yale), 4:331–41. See Dwight, *Works*, 1:171–86, for Sarah's account; and Samuel Frank Child, *A Puritan Wooing* (New York: Baker and Taylor, 1898), 103–14, for a fictional one. For critical appraisals, see Amanda Porterfield, *Feminine Spirituality in America: From Sarah Edwards to Martha Graham* (Philadelphia: Temple University Press, 1980), 39–48, and Julie Ellison, "The Sociology of 'Holy Indifference': Sarah Edwards' Narrative," *American Literature* 56 (December 1984): 479–95.

24. *Works* (Yale), 4:353–58.

25. Thomas Prince published *The Christian History* weekly from 5 March 1743 to 23 February 1744/5.

26. *Great Concern* (Boston: Green, Bushell, and Allen, 1743); see *Works* (1829), 7:195.

27. *True Excellency* (Boston: Rogers and Fowle, 1744); see *Works* (1808), 8:365 and 373.

28. *The Church's Marriage* (Boston: S. Kneeland and T. Green, 1746); see *Works* (1808), 8:324.

29. The first is *Copies of the Two Letters* (Boston: S. Kneeland and T. Green, 1745); the second, *An Expostulary Letter* (Boston: S. Kneeland and T. Green, 1745).

30. *Religious Affections* (Boston: S. Kneeland and T. Green, 1746). Reprinted in *Religious Affections,* ed. John E. Smith, *The Works of Jonathan Edwards* (New Haven: Yale University Press, 1959), 2:84–461, it is divided in three parts: I, 93–124; II, 127–90; III, 193–461. Smith has written more recently on *Religious Affections*: besides his introduction (2:1–83), see "Jonathan Edwards: Piety and Practice in the American Character," *Journal of Religion* 54 (April 1974): 166–80; and "Testing the Spirits: Jonathan Edwards and the Religious Affections," *Union Seminary Quarterly Review* 37 (Fall 1981): 27–37.

31. A manuscript letter reprinted in *Works* (Yale), 5:48.

32. *Humble Attempt* (Boston: D. Henchman, 1748); reprinted in *Apocalyptic Writings,* ed. Stephen J. Stein, *The Works of Jonathan Edwards* (New Haven: Yale University Press, 1977), 5:308–436. See Stein's introductory remarks (5:1–93) for its provenance and its place in apocalyptic thought. For its influence on Baptists, missionaries, and ecumenism, see, respectively, Ernest A. Payne, "The Evangelical Revival and the Beginnings of the Modern Missionary Movement," *Congregational Quarterly* 21 (July 1943): 223–36; John Foster, "The Bicentenary of Jonathan Edwards' 'Humble Attempt,'" *International Review of Missions* 37 (October 1948): 375–81; and R. Pierce Beaver, "The Concert of Prayer for Missions: An Early Venture in Ecumenical Action," *Ecumenical Review* 10 (July 1958): 420–27.

33. Part I, *Works* (Yale), 5:314–28; II, 329–67; III, 368–431.

34. *Works* (Yale), 4:520.

35. *True Saints* (Boston: Rogers and Fowle, 1747); see *Works* (Yale), 7:551.

36. *Life of Brainerd* (Boston: D. Henchman, 1749); reprinted in *The Life of David Brainerd,* ed. Norman Pettit, *The Works of Jonathan Edwards* (New Haven: Yale University Press, 1985), 7:89–541: preface, 89–99; text, 99–499; appendix, 500–41. For Edwards's work on Brainerd's diaries and journals, see Pettit's introduction, 7:1–87; for a less charitable view, see Richard Ellsworth Day, *Flagellant on Horseback: The Life Story of David Brainerd* (Philadelphia: Judson Press, 1950), 171–201; and for its popularity, see Joseph Conforti, "Jonathan Edwards's Most Popular Work: 'The Life of David Brainerd' and Nineteenth-Century Evangelical Culture," *Church History* 54 (June 1985): 188–201.

37. *Works* (Yale), 7:508–9.

38. *A Strong Rod* (Boston: Rogers and Fowle, 1748); see *Works* (1808), 8:453–56.

39. *Humble Inquiry* (Boston: S. Kneeland, 1749); see *Works* (1808),

1:147–50. For an analysis of the change, see John F. Jamieson, "Jonathan Edwards's Change of Position on Stoddardeanism," *Harvard Theological Review* 74 (January 1981): 79–99.

40. Part I, *Works* (1808), 1:153–61; II, 152–258; III, 259–335.

41. *Works* (1808), 1:253.

Chapter 5

1. *Christ the Great Example* (Boston: T. Fleet, 1750); see *Works* (1808), 8:394. The sermon on John 13:15,16 was preached at Portsmouth, New Hampshire.

2. *Works* (1808), 1:141.

3. "Preface" to *True Religion Delineated* (Boston: S. Kneeland, 1750); see *The Great Awakening,* ed. C. C. Goen, *The Works of Jonathan Edwards* (New Haven: Yale University Press, 1972), 4:570.

4. *Sermons* (1780), 201–20; see *Works* (1808), 8:230 and 240.

5. Letter to John Erskine, 15 November 1750; see Dwight, *President Edwards,* 416, and Hopkins, *Life and Character,* 62. For the arrangements between the parish and Edwards after his dismissal, see Winslow, *Jonathan Edwards,* 366, n. 21.

6. *True Grace* (New York: James Parker, 1753); see *Works* (1808), 7:223, 255–58, and 266. For its place in the Edwards canon, see Carl W. Bogue, *Jonathan Edwards and the Covenant of Grace* (Cherry Hill, N. J.: Mack Publishing, 1975).

7. Preface to *Freedom of the Will,* ed. Paul Ramsay, *The Works of Jonathan Edwards* (New Haven: Yale University Press, 1957), 1:131 and 133.

8. For the Bellamy letter, 15 January 1741, see Stanley T. Williams, "Six Letters of Jonathan Edwards to Joseph Bellamy," *New England Quarterly* 1 (April 1928): 228–32; for the Erskine letters, Dwight, *President Edwards,* 250, 251–52, 265–70, 405–13, 496–99, 507–12 and 533–34.

9. *Freedom of the Will* (Boston: S. Kneeland, 1754); reprinted in *Works* (Yale), 1:137–439. Printed in Schenectady and Wilmington, London and Liverpool, and translated into Dutch and Welsh, *Freedom of the Will* reached twenty editions in just over a hundred years. Critical commentary on Edwards's most famous treatise began early and shows no signs of letting up. See, for example, James Dana, *An Examination of the Late Reverend President Edwards's "Enquiry on Freedom of Will,"* 2 vols. (Boston: Daniel Kneeland, 1770) and (New Haven: Thomas and Samuel Green, 1773); Conrad Wright, "Edwards and the Arminians on the Freedom of the Will," *Harvard Theological Review* 35 (October 1942): 241–61; Arthur E. Murphy, "Jonathan Edwards on Free Will and Moral Agency," *Philosophical Review* 68 (April 1959): 181–202; W. P. Jeanes, "Jonathan Edwards's Conception of Freedom of the Will," *Scottish Journal of Theology* 14 (March 1961): 1–14; M. E. Grenander, "The Fourfold Way: Determinism, Moral Responsibility, and Aristotelian Causa-

tion," *Metamedicine* 3 (October 1982): 375–96; Arnold S. Kaufman and William K. Frankena, "Introduction," *Freedom of the Will* (Indianapolis: Bobbs-Merrill, 1969), ix–xxxviii; and, of course, Paul Ramsey's introduction, *Works* (Yale), 1:1–128. On the question of Arminianism, real or imagined, see Francis Albert Christie, "The beginnings of Arminianism in New England," in *Papers of the American Society of Church History,* 2nd series, ed. William Walker Rockwell (New York: G. P. Putnam's Sons, 1912), 3:151–72; and Gerald J. Goodwin, "The Myth of 'Arminian Calvinism' in Eighteenth-Century New England," *New England Quarterly* 41 (June 1968): 213–37.

10. *Works* (Yale), 1:464–65 and 470.

11. Part I, *Works* (Yale), 1:137–67; II, 171–273; III, 277–333; IV, 337–429; and Conclusion, 430–39.

12. *Works* (Yale), 1:345–46.

13. *Works* (Yale), 1:454.

14. *Works* (Yale), 1:172.

15. *Works* (Yale), 1:370.

16. *Original Sin* (Boston: S. Kneeland, 1758). Reprinted in *Works* (Yale), 3:102–437, it is divided in five parts: Part I, 107–219; II, 223–349; III, 353–71; IV, 375–433; and Conclusion, 434–37. *Original Sin* never gained the popularity of *Freedom of the Will*—the last of a dozen editions was published in 1837, one in Welsh following that—nor the critical notice. But see George Park Fisher, "The Augustinian and the Federal Theories of Original Sin Compared," *New Englander* 27 (July 1867): 468–516; David James Lyttle, "Jonathan Edwards on Personal Identity," *Early American Literature* 7 (Fall 1972): 163–71; Paul Helm, "Jonathan Edwards and the Doctrine of Temporal Parts," *Archiv für Geschichte der Philosophie* 61 (1979): 37–51; and C. Samuel Storms, *Tragedy in Eden: Original Sin in the Theology of Jonathan Edwards* (Lanham, Md.: University Press of America, 1985). Clyde A. Holbrook, the editor of the Yale edition, wrote a detailed account of the text in his introduction (1–101) and of its place in the neo-orthodox debate: "Jonathan Edwards Addresses Some 'Modern Critics' of Original Sin," *Journal of Religion* 63 (July 1983): 211–30.

17. Letter to John Erskine, 31 August 1748; see Dwight, *President Edwards,* 251. Edwards also acknowledges receipt of Taylor's *Key to the Apostolic Writings* with his *Paraphrase on the Epistle to the Romans* in the same packet, titles he cites in *Original Sin*. As well, Edwards cites other writers—Francis Hutcheson, John Locke, George Turnbull, and Henry Winder, among them—but far less often than Taylor.

18. Preface, *Works* (Yale), 3:102–4. In 1757, the year Edwards wrote *Original Sin,* the Rev. Samuel Webster published (in New Haven) *A Winter Evening's Conversation upon the Doctrine of Original Sin . . . Wherein the Notion of Our Having Sinned in Adam and Being on that Account Only Liable to Eternal Damnation, Is Proved To Be Unscriptural, Emotional, and of Dangerous Tendency.* The following year, five more pamphlets on the subject and the season ap-

peared: Peter Clark, *Scripture-Doctrine of Original Sin Stated and Defended. A Summer Morning's Conversation between a Minister and a Neighbor, a Reply to a Winter Evening's Conversation*; Webster, again, *The Winter's Conversation Vindicated*; Charles Chauncy, *The Opinion of One Who Has Perused the Summer Morning's Conversation*; Clark, again, *Remarks on a Late Pamphlet, Entitled the Opinion*; and Joseph Bellamy, *A Letter to the Reverend Author of the Winter-Evening's Conversation on Original Sin.*

19. *Works* (Yale), 3:253–54.

20. *Two Dissertations* (Boston: S. Kneeland, 1765); *True Virtue* is reprinted in *Works* (1808), 2:395–471. It was reprinted seven times over the next one hundred years, including translations into Dutch and Welsh. Criticism of it generally falls into two categories, aesthetics and influences. A good but difficult start on the first is Roland André Delattre, *Beauty and Sensibility in the Thought of Jonathan Edwards: An Essay in Aesthetics and Theological Ethics* (New Haven: Yale University Press, 1968); no less formidable on the second is Norman Fiering, *Jonathan Edwards's Moral Thought and Its British Context* (Chapel Hill: University of North Carolina Press, 1981). For other studies on Edwards's aesthetics (and ethics), see Rufus Suter, "The Concept of Morality in the Philosophy of Jonathan Edwards," *Journal of Religion* 14 (July 1934): 265–72; Sang Hyun Lee, "Mental Activity and the Perception of Beauty in Jonathan Edwards," *Harvard Theological Review* 69 (October 1976): 369–96; Terrence Erdt, *Jonathan Edwards, Art and the Sense of the Heart* (Amherst: University of Massachusetts Press, 1980); and William C. Spohn, S. J., "Sovereign Beauty: Jonathan Edwards and the Nature of True Beauty," *Theological Studies* 42 (September 1981): 394–421. For other source studies, see Alfred Owen Aldridge, "Edwards and Hutcheson," *Harvard Theological Review* 44 (January 1951): 35–53; Perry Miller, "Sinners in the Hands of a Benevolent God," in his *Nature's Nation* (Cambridge, Mass.: Harvard University Press, 1967), 279–89; Paul J. Nagy, "Jonathan Edwards and the Metaphysics of Consent," *Personalist* 51 (Autumn 1970): 434–46; and Emily Stipes Watts, "The Neoplatonic Basis of Jonathan Edwards' 'True Virtue,'" *Early American Literature* 10 (Fall 1975): 179–89. William K. Frankena edited a paperback text (Ann Arbor: University of Michigan Press, 1960) with an introduction, v–xiii.

21. In an appendix to his *An Inquiry into the Nature of True Holiness* (Newport, R.I.: Solomon Southwick, 1773), Samuel Hopkins answers William Hart, *Remarks on President Edwards's Dissertation concerning the Nature of True Virtue* (New Haven: T. & S. Green, 1771); Moses Hemenway, *A Vindication of the Power, Obligation and Encouragement of the Unregenerate to Attend the Means of Grace* (Boston: J. Kneeland, 1772); and Moses Mather, *The Visible Church in Covenant with God* (New Haven: T. & S. Green, 1770).

22. For suggestive continuities, see, among others, Perry Miller, "From Edwards to Emerson," *New England Quarterly* 13 (December 1940): 589–617, and Mason Lowance, Jr., "From Edwards to Emerson to Thoreau: A Reval-

uation," *American Transcendental Quarterly,* no. 18, parts 1–2 (Spring 1973): 3–12.

23. Reprinted in *Works* (1808), 6:9–124. Criticism about *The End of Creation* itself is sparse and widely scattered; see Edward Beecher, "Man in the Image of God," *Bibliotheca Sacra* 7 (July 1850): 409–25, and William C. Wisner, "The End of God in Creation," *American Biblical Repository* 6 (July 1850): 430–56; and George S. Hendry, "The Glory of God and the Future of Man," *Reformed World* 34 (December 1976): 147–57.

24. *Works* (1808), 6:12.

Chapter 6

1. Reuben A. Holden, *Yale: A Pictorial History* (New Haven: Yale University Press, 1967), plate 212.

2. *Jonathan Edwards: Representative Selections,* ed. Clarence H. Faust and Thomas H. Johnson (New York: American Book Co., 1935); Thomas H. Johnson, *The Printed Writings of Jonathan Edwards 1703–1758: A Bibliography* (Princeton, N.J.: Princeton University Press, 1940); Ola Elizabeth Winslow, *Jonathan Edwards, 1703–1758: A Biography* (New York: Macmillan Co., 1940); *Images or Shadows of Divine Things,* ed. Perry Miller (New Haven: Yale University Press, 1948); Perry Miller, *Jonathan Edwards* (New York: William Sloane Associates, 1949); *The Philosophy of Jonathan Edwards from His Private Notebooks,* ed. Harvey G. Townsend (Eugene, Ore.: University of Oregon Press, 1955); and Jack Duncan Coombe, *Consider My Servant* (New York: Exposition Press, 1957).

3. William S. Morris wrote the article, *New England Quarterly* 30 (December 1957): 515–25; Henry Banford Parkes wrote the book (New York: Minton, Balch, 1930). For other assessments of Edwards's changing reputation, see Clyde A. Holbrook, "Jonathan Edwards and His Detractors," *Theology Today* 10 (October 1953): 384–96; Daniel B. Shea, "Jonathan Edwards: The First Two Hundred Years," *Journal of American Studies* 14 (August 1980): 181–97; Donald Weber, "The Figure of Jonathan Edwards," *American Quarterly* 35 (Winter 1983): 556–64; and M. X. Lesser, "Introduction," *Jonathan Edwards: A Reference Guide* (G. K. Hall, 1981), xiii–lix, from which much of this chapter is drawn.

4. Beecher's comment is found in *Autobiography, Correspondence, Etc. of Lyman Beecher, D. D.,* ed. Charles Beecher (New York: Harper and Bros., 1865), 2:238; his wife's, in Lyman Beecher Stowe, *Saints, Sinners and Beechers* (Indianapolis: Bobbs-Merrill, 1934), 46.

5. Johnson's remarks are found in *The Life of Samuel Johnson* (London: Charles Dilly, 1790), 2:227–28; Emerson's in his *Journals,* ed. Edward Waldo Emerson and Waldo Emerson Forbes (Boston: Houghton Mifflin, 1909), 1:286–87; and Twain's in his *Letters,* ed. Albert Bigelow Paine (New York: Harper, 1917), 2:719–21.

6. Such comments were typical; for these, see Samuel J. Baird, "Edwards and the Theology of New England," *Southern Presbyterian Review* 10 (January 1858): 576–92; W. E. H. Lecky, *History of the Rise and Influence of the Spirit of Rationalism in Europe* (New York: D. Appleton, 1868), 1:368; and W. Ellerby, "Editor's Preface" (London: Longmans, 1817), iii–viii.

7. See George M. Marsden, *The Evangelical Mind and the New School Presbyterian Experience: A Case Study of Thought and Theology in Nineteenth-Century America* (New Haven: Yale University Press, 1970), 31–36, 177–79; for Edwards's relevance to today's evangelicals, see Martin E. Marty, "The Edwardean Tradition," *Christian Century* 91 (January 2, 1974): 18, 20–31. For the effect of *Humble Attempt* and *Life of Brainerd* on the missionary movement, see Ernest A. Payne, "The Evangelical Revival and the Beginnings of the Modern Missionary Movement," *Congregational Quarterly* 21 (July 1943): 223–36.

8. *Fraser's Magazine,* n.s. 8 (November 1873): 529–51; *Jonathan Edwards* (Boston: Houghton Mifflin, 1889).

9. Frank Hugh Foster, *A Genetic History of New England Theology* (Chicago: University of Chicago Press, 1907), 47–103; Jan Ridderbos, *De Theologie van Jonathan Edwards* (The Hague: Johan A. Nederbragt, 1907); and I. Woodbridge Riley, "Jonathan Edwards," in his *American Philosophy: The Early Schools* (New York: Dodd, Mead), 126–87.

10. *Encyclopaedia Britannica* (1910), 9:5, and (1929), 8:20.

11. *Jonathan Edwards* (New York: William Sloane, 1949). For his signal importance, see Donald Weber, "Perry Miller and the Recovery of Jonathan Edwards," introductory to a reissue of the text (Amherst: University of Massachusetts Press, 1981), v–xxiv.

12. Conrad Cherry, *The Theology of Jonathan Edwards: A Reappraisal* (Garden City, N.Y.: Doubleday, 1966); Norman Fiering, *Jonathan Edwards's Moral Thought and Its British Context* (Chapel Hill: University of North Carolina Press, 1981).

13. Andrew Hudgins, "Awaiting Winter Visitors: Jonathan Edwards, 1749," 46; Mary Ann Waters, "Sermon for Jonathan Edwards," 218.

Bibliography of Primary Sources

INDIVIDUAL WORKS

An Account of the Life of the Late Reverend Mr. David Brainerd, Minister of the Gospel, Missionary to the Indians, from the honorable Society in Scotland, for the Propagation of Christian Knowledge, and Pastor of a Church of Christian Indians in New-Jersey. Boston: D. Henchman, 1749.

A careful and strict Enquiry Into The modern prevailing Notions Of That Freedom of Will, Which is supposed to be essential To Moral Agency, Vertue and Vice, Reward and Punishment, Praise and Blame. Boston: S. Kneeland, 1754.

Charity And Its Fruits; Or, Christian Love As Manifested In the Heart And Life. London: James Nisbet, 1852.

Christ the great Example of Gospel Ministers. Boston: T. Fleet, 1750.

The Church's Marriage to her Sons, and to her God. Boston: S. Kneeland and T. Green, 1746.

Copies of the Two Letters Cited by the Rev. Mr. Clap. Boston: S. Kneeland and T. Green, 1745.

Discourses on Various Important Subjects, Nearly concerning the great Affair of the Soul's Eternal Salvation. Boston: S. Kneeland and T. Green, 1738.

The Distinguishing Marks Of a Work of the Spirit of God. Applied to that uncommon Operation that has lately appeared on the Minds of many of the People of this Land: With a particular Consideration of the extraordinary Circumstances with which this Work is attended. Boston: S. Kneeland and T. Green, 1741.

A Divine and Supernatural Light, Immediately imparted to the Soul by the Spirit of God, Shown to be both a Scriptural, and Rational Doctrine; In a Sermon Preach'd at Northampton, And Published at the Desire of some of the Hearers. Boston: S. Kneeland and T. Green, 1734.

An Expostulary Letter from the Rev. Mr. Edwards of Northampton, To The Rev. Mr. Clap. Boston: S. Kneeland and T. Green, 1745.

A Faithful Narrative Of The Surprising Work of God In The Conversion of Many Hundred Souls in Northampton, and the Neighboring Towns and Villages of the County of Hampshire, in the Province of the Massachusetts-Bay in New-England. Boston: S. Kneeland, T. Green, and D. Henchman, 1738.

A Farewel-Sermon Preached at the first Precinct in Northampton, After the People's publick Rejection of their Minister, and renouncing their Relation to Him as Pastor of the Church there, on June 22. 1750. Occasion'd by Difference of Sentiments, concerning the requisite Qualifications of Members of the Church, in compleat Standing. Boston: S. Kneeland, 1751.

God Glorified in the Work of Redemption, By the Greatness of Man's Dependence upon Him, in the Whole of it. Boston: S. Kneeland and T. Green, 1731.

The Great Christian Doctrine of Original Sin defended; Evidences of it's Truth produced, And Arguments to the Contrary answered. Boston: S. Kneeland, 1758.

The great Concern of A Watchman For Souls, appearing in the Duty he has to do, and the Account he has to give, represented and improved. Boston: Green, Bushell, and Allen, 1743.

A History Of the Work of Redemption. Containing, The Outlines of a Body of Divinity, In a Method entirely new. Edinburgh: W. Gray, 1774.

An Humble Attempt To promote Explicit Agreement and Visible Union of God's People in Extraordinary Prayer For the Revival of Religion and the Advancement of Christ's Kingdom on Earth, pursuant to Scripture-Promises and Prophecies concerning the last time. Boston: D. Henchman, 1748.

An Humble Inquiry Into the Rules of the Word of God Concerning The Qualifications Requisite to a Compleat Standing and full Communion In the Visible Christian Church. Boston: S. Kneeland, 1749.

Images or Shadows of Divine Things, edited by Perry Miller. New Haven: Yale University Press, 1948.

Miscellaneous Observations On Important Theological Subjects, Original and Collected. Edinburgh: M. Gray, 1793.

Misrepresentations Corrected, And Truth vindicated. Boston: S. Kneeland, 1752.

"Personal Narrative" in *The Life and Character Of The Late Reverend Mr. Jonathan Edwards, President of the College at New-Jersey* [by Samuel Hopkins]. Boston: S. Kneeland, 1765.

Practical Sermons, Never Before Published. Edinburgh: M. Gray, 1788.

"Preface," *True Religion Delineated,* by Joseph Bellamy. Boston: S. Kneeland, 1750.

The Resort and Remedy of those that are bereaved by the Death of an eminent Minister. Boston: G. Rogers, 1741.

Sermons on The Following Subjects. Hartford: Hudson and Goodwin, 1780.

Sinners In the Hands of an Angry God. A Sermon Preached at Enfield, July 8th 1741. At a Time of great Awakenings; and attended with remarkable Impressions on many of the Hearers. Boston: S. Kneeland and T. Green, 1741.

Some Thoughts Concerning the present Revival of Religion In New-England, And the Way in which it ought to be acknowledged and promoted, Humbly offered to the Publick, in a Treatise on that Subject. In Five Parts. Boston: S. Kneeland and T. Green, 1743.

A Strong Rod broken and withered. Boston: Rogers and Fowle, 1748.

A Treatise Concerning Religious Affections, In Three Parts. Boston: S. Kneeland and T. Green, 1746.

The True Excellency of a Minister of the Gospel. Boston: Rogers and Fowle, 1744.

True Grace, Distinguished from the Experience of Devils. New York: James Parker, 1753.

True Saints, when absent from the Body, are present with the Lord. Boston: Rogers
  and Fowle, 1747.
*Two Dissertations, I. Concerning the End for which God created the World. II. The
  Nature of True Virtue.* Boston: S. Kneeland, 1765.
*An Unpublished Essay Of Edwards On the Trinity With Remarks On Edwards And
  His Theology,* by George P. Fisher. New York: Charles Scribner's Sons,
  1903.

COLLECTED WORKS

The Works of Jonathan Edwards, edited by Perry Miller and John E. Smith.
  New Haven: Yale University Press, 1957–.
The Works of President Edwards, In Eight Volumes, edited by Samuel Austin.
  First American Edition. Worcester: Isaiah Thomas, 1808–1809.
The Works of President Edwards: With a Memoir Of His Life, In Ten Volumes, edited
  by Sereno E. Dwight. New York: S. Converse, 1829–30.

Index